The Traditional Music of Kashmir

In Relation to Indian Classical Music

DR. SUNITA DHAR
Head & Dean
Faculty of Music & Fine Arts.
University of Delhi

KANISHKA PUBLISHERS, DISTRIBUTORS
New Delhi-110002

KANISHKA PUBLISHERS, DISTRIBUTORS
4697/5-21A, Ansari Road, Daryaganj
New Delhi -110 002
Phones : 2327 0497, 2328 8285
Fax : 011-2328 8285
E-mail : kanishka_publishing@yahoo.co.in

The Traditional Music of Kashmir:
In Relation to Indian Classical Music
First Published 2003
Edition-2019

ISBN: 978-81-7391-553-9

PRINTED IN INDIA

Published by Madan Sachdeva for Kanishka Publishers, Distributors, 4697/5-21A, Ansari Road, Daryaganj, New Delhi-110 002, Typeset by Sunshine Graphics, Delhi, and Printed at Rajdhani Printers, Delhi.

Dedicated to
my dear mother
Late Smt. Indrawati Chowdhary
whose values, noble deeds,
sublime qualities and beliefs will
always serve as a beacon
of light to us.

Foreword

All reference to the historical, social and cultural aspects of Kashmir normally begins and ends with the Nilamat Purana and Pandit Kathana's Rajtarangini. Thanks to the concentrated effort of Dr. Sunita Dhar (Dean, Faculty of Music and Fine Arts, University of Delhi), another treatise has been added to the distinguished list of references. The book 'The Traditional Music of Kashmir—In Relation to Indian Classical Music' could not have come at a better time today, when a culturally rich state has been stripped of its glory by terrorism, the return of democracy is but a first step on the journey to normalcy. It is only when society prospers that culture can also develop. Hopefully, this book is a harbinger of the return of good times, when the lush valleys will once again resonate with the melody of pastoral tunes, when the bountiful earth shall thrum with dancing feet and the air shall vibrate with an energy only music can generate. Music knows no language, for it is an expression of the spirit and the soul. It transcends all barriers and brings people together. May the land of Kashmir be blessed again.

Prof. Sumati Mutatkar

Preface

Kashmir has consistently enjoyed a rich and distinct cultural heritage that has been always viewed with awe in the Indian horizon. The social, cultural, economic and artistic life of the people in this "Paradise upon earth" inspired many writers and researchers (including me) to choose subjects varied in nature reflecting the cultural legacy of the land. Kalhana's 'Rajtarangini' is one of the works, which brought into limelight several such nuances of the lives of the people of Kashmir to write on the subjects, which had a social and cultural bearing.

My book focuses on the subject "Traditional music of Kashmir in relation to Indian classical music". Music is basically a spontaneous creation, which gives expression to human instincts, sentiments and emotions with its universal appeal and potentiality to enlighten the soul. It has been the most important medium of expressing to human emotions from early stages of life on earth. This art has progressed and evolved everywhere in the world with the evolution of civilizations. Different places and different nations have evolved their different forms of music and art. Wherever human civilization and culture advanced, literature learning and art got promoted. The advancement in civilization from time to time have witnessed simultaneous progress, development and promotion of music.

Delving into the past brought me to the conclusion that the music of Kashmir during the Hindu period was more or less a shadow of Indian Music. Nilmatpurana and Kalhana's chronicle suggest that ancient music of Kashmir was a version of Indian music. Ancient Kashmir had been a prominent center for learning of art and the courts were thronged by artists and musicians. They maintained very close links with the rest of the country and Indian impression was reflected in the culture of this place. The art of writing on the subject of music had not been in vogue. The musicians and artists did not relish writing during those days, as a result of which we do not possess any written material on the notation or on the grammar of music, which was prevalent at that time. Kashmiri have been great lovers of music. Since Kashmiri language does not have any script of its own, the culture and tradition preserved in its music has passed from generation to generation.

However some styles of music and singing like temple sangeet, Shiv *gayan* and folk music survived the upheavals and persisted to appeal on account of their sentimental value and emotional attachment. These styles of music are continuing even now as a distinct genre and as a tradition of ancient Kaṣhmir. Kashmiri music is so full of melody and rhythm that it distinguishes itself easily from the music of any other state. The delicacy, the grace and charm of Kashmiri music is ultimate.

There is no function or celebration which is performed without music. Not only on happy occasions but even in times of sorrow, the involvement of music is a must. Like 'Van', a folk form of Kashmir that is sung when someone dies and an environment of sadness prevails all over. It is a matter of honour for the Kashmiris that Lalleshwari, Habba Khatoon, etc. the great musical personalities belonged to Kashmir. Lalleshwari—the mystic poetess who used to roam naked—was of the opinion that the body is a creation of God and so need not be covered. Her couplets were superb and people even after years find solace in her poetry. Her 'Vakhs' are sung in every Kashmiri family. Likewise Habba-Khatoon's invention of Ragas, poetry have all gone a long way in building the culture of Kashmir.

Although the Kashmiris came under the threat of losing their art and culture by the militants even then the modern institution of culture and art, media, electronic media, cultural academy and Information Department of J&K Government have played a key role for revival of the art and initiated serious efforts for preserving and promoting the invaluable cultural heritage. These institutions are credited with strenuous efforts endeavouring at a suitable notation system, appropriate grammar and development of audio-visual aids.

In the present study, the traditional music of Kashmir has been divided into the following categories:

1. Songs sung by women folk
2. Songs sung by minstrels
3. Songs sung by the professionals with the view of earning money
4. Songs sung by farmers
5. Religious songs : Bhajan, Leela, Shiva songs.

Songs sung by Women Folk

Vanvun is a prayer in the form of folk music. It commences with a prayer to God. The subjects of vanvun also refer to the events of the Vedic period. In Vedic period, when Goddess Sinnavali's marriage was performed, God Pooshan had prepared a beautiful headgear to decorate her head. This was called Kapal—apush in Sanskrit. Lord Indra beautified it further, wrapping a white strip of cloth around it. This custom prevails among Kashmiris as a compulsory item of marriage even today. 'Kalpush' in Kashmiri, is Kapal-Push in Sanskrit and the white twinkling strip is Tarang in Kashmiri. The customs till date are followed accordingly.

In the pronunciation of Vedic language with the use of Uddatta, Anudatta and Swarit, every vowel and its following consonant preserves its pronouncing capacity. The technique with which Uddata, Anudatta and Swarit are used for modulation in chanting of Vedas, is the same as used in vanvun singing.

Vanvun played a leading role in maintaining the continuity of our culture from the Vedic period through the Ramayana, Mahabharata and Shrimata Bhagwat till the present day. Hindu Vanvun preserves our faith in spiritual and ancient beliefs; besides it provides religious fervour and divine grace to the occasions as we welcome Lord Siva and Parvati to participate at the outset of every ceremony. The fact is that the Kashmiri language, cultures as well as religious ceremonies have a direct bearing on the speakers of Rigvedic language. Vanvun thus, is the pure reflection of the same.

Ruf: Ruf is a very interesting and emotional type of folk dance. It is directly related with spring. Every season lasts for three months. At the outset of spring, Kashmiri entertain themselves by dancing and singing. This practice was prevalent even in the ancient time, which is mentioned in Nilamatapurana.

Hikat: It is an inseparable part of 'raas'. We can even call it a form of 'raas'. Reference of 'raas' is prevalent in Kashmir, and is available in Bhatt Avatar. Even his predecessor, Nund Rishi, was acquainted with 'raas'. In this dance two girls stand in a circle in a pair, facing each other with two sticks in each hand and strike at each other's stick and sing.

Lalnavun: In Hindi it is called 'Lori', in English it is called Lullaby and in Kashmiri it is called Lalnavun. Lalnavun is based on Vatsalaya Ras. It reflects motherly love, which is pure. It depicts the unbroken bond between the mother and the child. The Mother prays for the long life of the child and to make the child sleep.

Songs sung by the Minstrels

These songs are sung by the professionals from the view of earning money. They sing Band Pather, Ladishah, Chhakri.

Chhakri—one of the many forms of folk music of Kashmir—is rhythmic, fast and when in full swing attracts the attention of each and every listener. The environment around gets totally melodious and musical and people start dancing. Likewise 'Ruf' another folk form of Kashmir is mainly a dance item. Ruf has been derived from the word *dwarf*, which means a black bee. As the black bee sucks the juice of the flower, sits on it, moves forward and goes backward, the same moment has been depicted in Ruf dance.

Chhakar has an important place in the Kashmiri folk music. This type of song has been practiced for a long time. It is sung collectively in a group and the singers, themselves play the instruments and the style of singing is such that the first line of the song is sung by the leading singer. The same line is repeated by other members of the group. It is a very popular and entertaining folk song.

Bachhi Nagma: The general meaning of the Bachhi Nagma is adolescent melodious voice. But in villages, it is still known by the old name 'bachhi gyavun'. During the Pathan reign (1758-1818) the Arabic word 'nagma' must have been added to it. So it is the mixture of bachhi (originated from Sanskrit) and 'nagma' (originated from Arabic). Their dress matches the dress of kathak dancers. The Kashmiris have great liking for the dance and music of Bachhi Nagma.

Dhamaly means leaping and jumping. Dhamaly is a holy sport in Brij in Uttar Pradesh. It is related with an exercise of saints who jump over burning fire. This is a dance performed by fifteen to twenty persons. Ladies don't take part in it. The whole team wears white cotton dress and a head gear.

Songs sung by the Farmers

Naind Gyavun: This song is related to farmers' folk songs. 'Ninad' of Sanskrit. The word Gyavun is originated from 'Gayan' of Sanskrit. The tradition of agricultural songs is prevalent in every state and region. The nature of agricultural songs is joyful, exciting and merry making. Songs make difficult tasks of the farmers easy and enhances their zeal.

Religious Songs

Leela songs are dedicated to God. Prayer songs in Kashmiri were written in Sanskrit in the past which were dedicated to Shiv Shakti, Vishnu and Budh Dharam. Kashmir has been the place of Rishis whose every action was consecrated to spiritual powers. Even today we can hear Hindus in temples reciting the couplets from 'Panchastavi' (prayer book in Sanskrit).

The first chapter defines the ancient Kashmir in its historical perspective. It gives an overview of the ups and downs that Kashmir witnessed.

The 2nd chapter delves into the origin and development of the music of Kashmir.

Kashmiri traditional music is blessed with melodious charm. Besides that, it is a store house of the traditions of Kashmir.

3rd chapter gives various categories of traditional music prevalent in Kashmir. The examples, the meanings and the occasions on which they are sung have been given i.e. Ruf, Vanvun. Marriage, Yagneopavit etc. Chhakri Lalnavun, Bandh Paether, Bachha Nagma Zarkaskasay, Hikat, Ladishah etc.

4th chapter presents some songs with their singing patterns by way of notations.

5th chapter presents some of the songs which have classical basis or are close to Ragas.

The last chapter deals with the instruments used to play with the traditional music of Kashmir.

The ancient history of Kashmir recorded by Pandit Kalhana in Rajtarangini has specifically mentioned the art of music and musical instruments in this region in the distant past. The ancient musical instruments used in Kashmir had been more or less a reflection of the Indian musical instruments in usage during that time. According to Pandit Kalhana, the folk musical instruments like earthern pots, brass vessels etc. were used by Kashmiri people from very early times. In the past Kashmiris used mainly rhythmic maintaining instruments like.

1. Tumbaknari
2. Noet
3. Setar
4. Nai (Flute)
5. Thaliz
6. Khayasa
7. Rabab
8. Santoor etc.

Among the musical instruments Santoor occupies an important place in Kashmiri music. Soofiana singing is not possible without the accompaniments. These days, it is gaining popularity even outside Kashmir. Its sweet tapping creates a feeling of romantic mood whereas its soft tunes remind of the tranquility of the other world, which suits the mystical temperament of Soofiana music. The instrument emits loud and enchanting sounds. Santoor is being used for Mousiqui in Kashmir since 13th century.

In the year 1956 the people of the state of J & K and around, heard for the first time, Indian Classical music being played by an artist on an instrument, which was restricted to Soofiana gayaki only. Kashmir is proud to produce eminent artists namely Pandit Bhajan Sopori, Tibbat Bakkal who have made a mark in the field of Hindustani Classical music and have greatly contributed their lot not only in Hindustani Classical music but have shown the relationship of Kashmiri music in Indian Classical music. Santoor, to his gharana is not only an instrument which produces enchanting tunes but an instrument that sings and is on par with Sitar, Sarod and Violin.

Pandit Sopori, as a Santoor player, has retained the traditions of santoor and the technical nuances essential for Indian Classical tradition.

Pt. Bhajan Sopori has composed music for Kashmiri serials like Heemal Nagrai and Habba khatoon etc.

In the end I would like to present some folk songs of Kashmir which are based on Indian ragas and talas, thus depicting the relationship of Kashmiri music to Hindustani Classical Music.

Dr. Sunita Dhar

Acknowledgements

I express my gratitude to the Higher Education Department, Government of J & K State, whose valuable suggestions helped me complete this work.

I owe a profound debt of gratitude to Ghulam Rasool Bhat Ex-Librarian (Curator), Research Library, University of J & K who took pains in reading and translating the Persian manuscripts. He also assisted me in tracing and utilizing these primary sources.

I am highly indebted to Mohammad Bhat who is the Kashmiri writer possessing relevant knowledge on the subject and his original contribution to traditional music is notable.

I owe my gratitude to the library of Pamposh School, located in Pamposh Enclave, New Delhi for allowing me to use the rich literature of the culture of Kashmir, from time to time.

I thank the contributions of the monthly magazine "Koshur-Samachar" whose articles went a long way in providing me guidance about the traditional music of Kashmir.

I am deeply indebted to all those who have helped me in writing this book and supported me throughout this endeavour.

Since last year, I have met various musicologists, artists, journalists, scholars and several acquiantances and friends of Kashmir who all generously shared with me their memories of Culture & Folk Music of Kashmir. I owe special gratitude to them all.

I would also like to thank several Kashmiri media personalities whose expert and invaluable comments on Kashmiri music in prominent dailies and magazines have been quoted by me in this book.

Contents

1

Ancient Kashmir

The ancient history of Kashmir is shrouded in mystery. The legends and myths trace the ancient history and reveal some glimpses of pre-historic Kashmir. According to legends the valley of Kashmir was originally a deep vast lake. The oldest record of this legend is 'Nilmata-Purana' which has been quoted by Pandit Kalhana (Great poet and historian who lived in 12th century A.D.) Pandit Kalhana mentions in his Raj-Tarangini (written in 1148-1149 A.D.) that at the beginning of Kalpa (cycle of creation of the universe) the valley was a lake, hundreds of feet deep, called Satisara. This land in the womb of the Himalaya was filled with water and formed the lake of Sati. Sati is goddess Parvati or Durga who was the divine consort of Lord Shiva. This lake was the favourite resort of this goddess. The demon infested lake dates back to the Seventh Manavantra, and the chief of these water demons was Jalodbhava (who dwelt in that lake). The demons used to terrorize the Nagas (snakes who guarded the waters) and caused great devastation and distress to the inhabitants of neighbouring plains. The great sage Kashyap, the grandson of Lord Brahma, heard from his son Nila (a Naga himself) the stories of brutal oppression and misery of the people of Satisara. He resolved to rescue his progeny. The sage did a long penance to relieve the sufferings of the people and his prayer was granted. Pandit Kalhana's

Nilamata-Purana, which quotes that Brahma, Vishnu and Shiva, acted as the leaders of the gods and assisted Kashyapa in defeating Jalodbhava. It is stated that while fighting the gods took positions on the peaks of surrounding mountains but the demon Jalodbhava would lived deep inside and hide himself in the womb of the water.

He refused to emerge and was invisible as long as he remained hidden. Goddess Sharika appeared in the form of Hari (a myna) carrying a pebble in her beak which she dropped upon Jalodbhava to finally slay him. The pebble is believed to be the hillock presently known as Hari Parbat or Sharika Parbat. The pleased Sage Kashyapa settled in the dry valley after the land and people were rescued from the dangers of demons. Kashmir is said to be named after this sage and it is believed that it was originally called Kashyap Mar (Mar meaning the habitant) which literally means settlement of Kashyapa. Other Gods and Goddesses were also so enchanted by the beauty of the valley that they also refused to leave.

According to Nilamata-Purana, names of places like Verinag, Anantnag, Sernag, Kokarnag etc. show traces of ancient Naga beliefs. After that people from South of India were settled by Kashyapa in the valley and the earliest settlers came from the Northern parts of Ladakh and Dardistan as well as from the plains of India. The earliest among the races that entered Kashmir from the Punjab and other parts of India were the Aryans.

According to Kalhana, history begins with King Gonanda I. After three Gonanda rulers twenty-three generations of Pandavas ruled over Kashmir. It is believed that 68 (sixty eight) kings of Gonanda dynasty ruled over Kashmir. They were weak and insignificant. Therefore, Ashoka extended his control over Kashmir. Ashoka is said to have built the towns of Srinagar on the bank of river Jhelum and has been responsible for introducing Buddhism in Kashmir. Buddhism did become the state religion in his reign, but he respected Hinduism as well. After his death, the Mauryan empire began to disintegrate and Jalika, Ashoka's son, became an independent monarch of Kashmir. Three centuries later, Kashmir passed under the control of Kushanas. Kanishka, Huska and Juska were among the well known Kushana rulers. Kanishka was the most powerful monarch, whose rule extended to North Western India and Central Asia. After Kushanas, Kashmir was ruled by a number of local rulers including Abhimanu, Vibhisana I, Inderjit, Ravana, Vibhisana II whose names occur in Ramayana. During the reign of these kings, Shaivism made headway. Kashmir was ruled over by the Huns for some time, but local rulers soon regained powers and the second Gonanda dynasty came into being.

After the fall of Gonanda dynasty Karkota dynasty established its rule in Kashmir. In all, sixteen kings of this dynasty ruled over the land for over two and a half centuries, some of whom played a prominent role in the expansion of economic, social, political, religious and cultural fields, beyond the frontier of the valley. Buddhism spread fairly well when Heiun-Tsang visited Kashmir and he noted remarkable religious tolerance.

Lalitaditya, known as Muktapida ruled over Kashmir, who was the most prominent king of the dynasty. After the fall of Karkota dynasty, Utpala dynasty came to power. One of the finest kings of this dynasty was Avantivarma. Never before were Kashmiris so happy and prosperous as during the twenty-eight years rule of Avantivarma who with the help of a local genius, Suyya, he founded the town of Avantipur and built two magnificent temples therein, namely Avantisvamin and Avantiswara. Hinduism gained prominence and Buddhism was relegated to the background.

Avantivarman's successor, Sankaravarman disturbed the peace and prosperity of the kingdom by resorting to unnecessary military expeditions. Then came the reign of

Gupta dynasty. After the Guptas came the rule of Kalsa and Harsa. Harsa was a remarkable figure, youthful and possessed great personal beauty. He was an expert linguist, a poet and highly educated. He was liberal and kind hearted. He had a taste for music. He composed songs and introduced Carnatak music to Kashmir. After him Jaya Simha ruled for twenty-eight years. After the death of Jaya Simha, Dulocha, a Mongol warrier and adventurer, who hailed from Turkistan, invaded Kashmir.

After the Buddhist rule, the events took such a turn that Kashmir witnessed the dawn of the Muslim Sultanate. Muslim rule started on a favourable note. Shah Mir adopted a human enlightenment and just approach. The next Sultan was Shahab-ud-din. Then came Qutub-ud-din. He banned un-Islamic practices like drinking, gambling, dancing and playing musical instruments. After his death, his son Zain-ul-abidin was the most tolerant and benevolent ruler. His reign was very peaceful. During his reign Hindu Mahabharta and Hindu Shastriyas were translated. He was a precursor of Akbar, in the field of religion and of Shah Jahan, in the field of construction. It was he, who developed the beautiful island, Char Chinari and the famous Dal lake.

In 1589, Kashmir became a province of the Mughal Empire. Akbar visited Kashmir in 1589. The Mughal institutions and Mughal pattern of administration were introduced. Jehangir, fell in love with Kashmir when he observed the beauty of a site near present day Gulmarg. His son, Shah Jahan made several trips to Kashmir. It was in Jehangir's and Shah Jahan's period that the world famous Mughal Gardens, including Shalimar, Nishatt, Achhabal, Chashma Shahi and Pari Mahal were developed.

During Aurangzeb's reign Kashmir saw fourteen governors.

After the death of Aurangzeb, Mughal empire began to crumble and Kashmir was destined to fall under the grip of the Afghans. Shah Abdali was invited to rule over the valley.

After that there was the beginning of Sikh rule in Kashmir which lasted for 20 years.

Dogra dynasty lasted for about hundred years. This period saw four Maharajas-Gulab Singh, Ranbir Singh, Pratap Singh and Hari Singh.

The Freedom Movement in India was gathering momentum and the Muslim league was emerging on the scene and these developments influenced events in the States of Jammu & Kashmir. A number of young men received higher education in Lahore and Aligarh and returned with a new political and social awakening. Sheikh Mohammad Abdullah was one of them. Today, the position has come to such a pass that majority of Hindus and some peace loving Muslims have migrated to other parts of India.

Origin of Music in Kashmir

Music is basically a spontaneous creation to give expression to human instincts, sentiments and emotions with its universal appeal and potentiality to enlighten soul. It has been the most important medium of expression of human emotions from early stages of life on earth. This art has progressed and evolved everywhere in the world with the evolution of civilizations. Different places and different nations have evolved their different music and art. Wherever human civilization and culture advanced, literature, learning and art got promoted. The advancements in civilization from time to time have witnessed simultaneous progress and promotion of music.

The kind, type and form of music that was in vogue in Kashmir in the distant past is unknown and unclear. Suitable techniques and art of writing on the subject of music had not been developed in ancient Kashmir. The musicians and artists did not also relish writing. Proper systems for teaching and learning this art had not been in use. During ancient times the people of Kashmir were the followers of Hinduism. This region was an abode of Hindu religion and people worshipped gods and deities, the which included worshipping of Shiva. The people were speaking Sanskrit dialect and hymns, lyrics, etc. were also sung in this language. The region was brought under the influence of Buddhism during the reign of Ashoka. However, no drastic change could take place in the spoken language, art, culture and music under the influence of the region. The only authoritative work, which traces the history of this early period, is Nilamata Purana which also contains references to music and art.

Many festivals were celebrated during this period in which musical concerts and dips in the river Vitasta, and collective singing in the evenings featured as per the details of Nilamata-Purana. There is no denying the fact that the art of music and dancing has been living in India from time immemorial. Mathura, Kashmir and Banaras had been the prominent centers of learning science and art. The temples used to be important places for learning music and singing and dancing girls used to perform in these temples. During this ancient Hindu rule one does not find any difference between the music, art and culture of Kashmir and that prevailing elsewhere in rest of India.

Kashmir has seen remarkable advancement and liberal patronage of music during this ancient period, which is clearly depicted by the tiles found during the excavations at Harwan. These tiles and some sculptures bear the pictures of dancing and singing persons and also of the ladies playing on the rhythmic instrument. The historical facts bear enough evidence that music and dancing had been popular in Kashmir in very old times.

Music and Fine Arts did not progress much during the 11th and 12th century A.D. This was the period of turmoil, disturbance and economic depression. The decadent state of Hindu rule for nearly two centuries resulted in their downfall. All the historians have consistently narrated that during the reign of Sukhdeva Kashmir was completely devastated by Dalacha who was a Tartar aggressor.

The ancient music that had survived subsequent to the invasion of Dalacha received another severe setback at the hands of Sultan Sikander. The period of this Sultan was predominated by an official attitude of hatred towards music and dance.

Srivara asserts that this Sultan on the provocation of some narrow-minded persons destroyed all the literature and material existent on the subject of music.

This means that Sultan Sikander under the influence of conservative Muslim priests had destroyed by setting on fire the religious books, Hindu manuscripts and the works on music and art. According to M.L. Kapur the musical instruments for entertainment purposes were forbidden by the Sultan. Thus the temple Sangit or the religious music got discouraged and was distanced from royal patronage.

The original faith of the people who lived in Kashmir valley was a sort of Shaivism. In the opinion of some scholars, Shiva shakti worship was prevalent in this region even before the advent of the Aryans to the Indian soil. It originated out of the cult of Mother Goddess and was closely connected with the cult of Shiva. The lamp of Shaivism burnt steadily in the valley throughout the period of Hindu rule and even afterwards. This gives a clear idea that Shiva Puja or worship of Shiva was generally practiced in Kashmir.

A renowned Shaivite school for teaching Kashmiri Shaivism and its philosophy is existent. An installation of this school was run by a well known Saint, Swami Laxman Jao, at Ishber, Srinagar. This saint is considered to be a reputed contemporary authority on Shaivism of Kashmir.

The language, civilization and culture of Central Asia cast its shadows on every walk of life in Kashmir. This was the time when the victories of Muslims had brought about changes in the language, civilizing music and art of the Indian subcontinent also. The new belief of Islam changed the lifestyle of the people in Kashmir like it had influenced the rest of India, particularly its northern parts. The music bloomed and came into vogue during the reign of Sultan Zain-ul-Abdin. Srivara was himself an accomplished artist and a great musician attached to the court of Sultan Hasan Shah. He was Head of the Department of Music and used to sing vernacular of Persian songs for the entertainment of the king and other countries in which he composed with leading musicians of that time. Sultan Zain-ul-Abidin and Sultan Hasan Shah have been in particular the luminaries for patronizing music and fine arts. They visited musicians from India and distant south. Their period is quite noticeable for overall progress. Music flourished and reached its climax under the patronage of the Sultan, whose court was adorned by renowned and prominent musicians brought from various distant places in India and Central Asia.

Sufi writes in the book *Kashir* that "he invited artists and musicians from Iran, Turan, Turkistan and Hindustan and offered them good prospects and concessions to settle down in Kashmir." In fact the main schools of music in the valley were founded by the Irani and Turani musicians in the time of Sultan Zain-ul-Abidin. During this period avenues were also found for adopting and including various Ragas and Raginis of Indian music.

Srivara writes that the singers from Karnataka sat gracefully before the king Hasan Shah as if they represented the six tunes namely Kedara, Gauda, Gandhara, Desha, Bangala and Malva. This makes it clear that serious efforts were made during this period for this entertaining fine art of music to reach the heights of perspective. Hence, the Indian musicians used to participate in the concert and competitions and would perform in the courts of the sultans for being generously awarded.

Sufi giving a vivid description states that when Muslims came over to India, they brought with them their own style, particularly Sufi music. Luminaries like Hazrat Amir Khusrau had made significant contributions for revamping the Indian music and bringing it closer to Central Asian and Persian music. It is quite reasonable to believe that Amir Khusrau had succeeded in his efforts to combine the Persian and Indian systems and evolve new melodies characteristic of the new personalized Indian Culture.

The new synthesis had come into vogue in India and was touching the heights of popularity. Thus, a synthesis was created which gave a vast scope to music for benefiting from certain concepts, experiments, achievements and fundamentals of Indian music. In the process, the music of Kashmir, which had primarily originated from the Central Asian and Persian music, was also shaping and evolving.

Folk music of Kashmir had been a spontaneous creation, associated with usual merry making celebrations and an automatic expression of joy and delight.

2

The Traditional Music of Kashmir

In the present study, the traditional music of Kashmir has been divided into the following categories:

1. Songs sung by women folk.
2. Songs sung by minstrel.
3. Songs sung by farmers.
4. Religious songs.

SONGS SUNG BY WOMEN FOLK

Vanvun, Veegyavachan, Van, etc. are some of the folk songs sung by the women folk of Kashmir. Such types of songs are sung at the time of festivals, marriages, etc. and even at the time of death. The lullaby, which is sung all over the world, is also sung by the women of Kashmir by the name of Lalnavun. Another type of music is Hikkachi, where the girls in Kashmir get together and sing. Such songs are full of love, affection and warmth.

Vanvun

Vanvun played a leading role in maintaining the continuity of our culture from the vedic period through the Ramayana, the Mahabharata and Shrimata Bhagwat, till the present day. Hindu Vanvun preserves our faith in spiritual and ancient beliefs. Besides, it provides religious fervour and divine grace to the occasions as we welcome Lord Shiva and Parvati to participate at the outset of every ceremony.

> शोकलं करिथ वनवुन ह्योतये
> शोभफल ह्युतये माजि भवानी।

Meaning : Vanvun is a prayer in the form of folk music. It commences with a prayer to God. The results are obviously auspicious, blessed by mother goddess Bhawani. Not only this, the subjects of Vanvun also refer to the events of the Vedic period. The customs till date are followed accordingly. For example, in Vedic period, when Goddess Sinnavali's marriage was performed. God Poosha had prepared a beautiful headgear to decorate her head. This was called 'Kapal-apush' in Sanskrit. Lord Indra, beautifying it further, had wrapped a white strip of cloth around it. This custom prevails among Kashmiris as a compulsory item of marriage even today. 'Kalpush', in Kashmiri, is 'Kapal-apush' in Sanskrit and the white twinkling strip is 'tarang-kor' in Kashmiri.

This ancient reality, which might have been forgotten in five thousand years, is alive in the following lines:

> पूशन थोवनय शनिवालि दी वी
> चे कूरि थोवनय मऽल्य माले।

Meaning: Vedic God Pushan himself prepared 'Kapal-apush' and decorated it for the head of Sinnavali, but in your case, your father and mother have put it on your head.

The above mentioned lines have been addressed to the bride. Researches are proving the fact that the Kashmiri language, culture as well as religious ceremonies have a direct bearing on the speakers of Rig-Vedic language. Vanvun, thus, is the pure reflection of the same and has been preserving the language and culture for generations to come. In the pronunciation of Vedic language with the use of uddatta, anudatta and swarit, every vowel and its following consonant preserves its pronouncing capacity.

The wonderful thing is that the technique with which uddatta, anudatta are used for modulation in chanting of Vedas, is the same as used in Vanvun singing. It is proved today that this style originated four thousand years ago.

Muslims have separated themselves from Hindus in their style of Vanvun singing. Among Kashmiri Hindus, a medium tone is used. It is sung in chorus form. Its soothing melody envelops the whole atmosphere with continuous peace and religious fervour. There is no element of tribal music in it. Both Hindus and Muslims use the same poetry, but the former use the classical mode and the latter the tribal. Muslims change words here and there to separate it from Hindu Vanvun. They sing fast and sometimes very fast. The examples of both are given below:

Hindu pattern of singing (with the use of uddatta, anudatta and swarit):

ते.......लि.......कौ.......नु.......आ.......यो.......ख.......सा.......नि.......
स.......आं.......गु.......न.......च.......ये.......ले.......
अ.......सि.......सो.......न.......ओ.......स.......पें.......
ठ.......शे.......रे.......स

Meaning: O son-in-law and his father, why did you not come, where we held a gold crown on our heads?

Muslim pattern of singing:

तेलि कौनु आयोख सऽनिस बाज़रस
येलि असि सॉन ओस दस्तारस।

Meaning: O son-in-law and his father, why did you not come, when we had gold on our 'dastar' (headgear)?

Among Hindus, vanvun performers sit in a round, pentagon, hexagon or nonagon form and sing vanvun, suiting the ceremony. First line is sung by some respectable old woman (sometimes, a professional singer), who sits on a slightly higher pedestal. The line is repeated by other women. The alleviation of the tone of the singing pattern is maintained throughout its singing, in accordance with the modulation, according to uddatta, anudatta and swarit avarohana.

The series of Hindu vanvun begins from the time when a girl expects a child and during sixth and seventh month of her conceiving. When she carries curd and other gifts to her in-laws. This ceremony is called "Pyav" in Kashmiri language. Milk and curd are considered to be auspicious in Kashmir. Then on the seventh or eighth day after the delivery, a social function is held. It is called 'Shran-sunder' (bath beauty). During the function, a birch leaf is lighted and a folk dance is organized, where 'Shokt pansund' is repeated that means dynasty may again be blessed with a son.

It is followed by singing vanvun:

थन येलि प्योहम रनुं–प्यव करमय
ज्योतशन त पंडितन कोरमय साल।

Meaning: As you were born, I cooked delicacies in lots and invited palmists and pandits.

Or

व्यनायक चोरम आथवार दरमय
कोरमय छ़ाँडदिथ शूबिदार नाव।

Meaning: For your birth, I observed fast on the fourth day of Vinayaka, which fell on Sunday. After your birth, I made a thorough search and got an auspicious name for you.

After the birth ceremony, comes "Zarkasaya" (Mundan). Zarkasaya is originated from Jatanishkasan in Sanskrit, i.e. removing hair and making the child bald.

रुत साथ वुछिथ जर हो कासय
आयिदरि बडिं बागि वनुवान छेय।

Meaning: After choosing a pious day, it was decided to remove your locks. We are singing vanvun for blessing you. O live long child.

In Kashmir, the hair of only the boy child is removed. On the eleventh day, after the birth of the child, another ceremony *Kahanaethur* is held. It is christening of the newly born. Yagya is performed. The infant is placed near it and he or she is made to taste pure ghee or honey. This way the impurity of birth is driven away. Parents embrace the child, give a peck on its forehead and welcome with flower petals.

बृहस्कथाए छांड दिथकोडयो
नाबो चोनुय शूबेदार
नावस चेनिस सोन मोख्त जरयो
नाव चोनुय शूबेदार

Meaning: I have made a thorough study of 'Brahaskatha' (Book of palmistry) for choosing a name for you. Your name is thus, a blessed one. I will set gold and pearls on your name.

The quantity of Hindu vanvun poetry is much more than that of Muslims.

An important ceremony that follows is yagnopavit, known, in Kashmiri, as 'mekhal'. In present times, Vanvun singing is not prevalent in the above mentioned ceremonies. It has two reasons: first, Vanvun singing is not possible by every woman of Kashmir. Secondly, due to the ignorance of its historical and spiritual value, people spare no time to sit and enjoy Vanvun singing. But 'mekhal' and marriages are not possible without Vanvun even today. On these occasions, the old women, who have the proficiency, and are in demand, enhance the grace, by their performance.

Kashmiri 'mekhal' and marriage ceremony-vanvun can be divided under ten headings:

1. Garnavaya (house cleaning and washing).
2. Dapun (personal invitation of guests for the approaching function).
3. Manzirath (henna dye and night singing).

4. Kroor (after a white wash flowery decoration at the main door).
5. Shran (sitting on stool and dripping milk, curd and bathing).
6. Devgun (welcome to Vedic Gods).
7. Varidan (gifts to the relatives).
8. Yonya (holy fire).
9. Tekya Narivan (holy mark on the forehead and sacred thread tied around the wrist).
10. Kalash Lava (after the worship of Kalash, sprinkling of water).

Garnavaya Vanavun

आकाशि प्यठे येलि गंगा द्राये
सूत्य छिस कारण तु दीवैयलूख
अछरछु वनुबुअन पतपत द्राये
हर गंगाये नमस्कार

Meaning: I salute the Ganga, which originated from the locks of Lord Shiva. While proceeding towards the earth, Brahma, Vishnu and Triloki lords accompanied Ganga. Ganga was followed by fairies from the heaven singing melodious song. I salute that Ganga, which flows from the locks of Lord Shiva.

Dapun Vanvun

After house cleaning, the lady of the house goes to her parents' home. A big feast is organised by her parents, when she goes to invite them.

दपनस क्युथये रथ मंगनोवमय
साथ नशिथुरु वुछुनोवमय,
दीवकी माजिक्युथ रथ मंगनोवमय
साथ नशिथुरु वुछुनोवमय,
महाराज दीवन होस मंगनोवमय,
हस्तिय स्वपन साज़ करनोवमय
तथि प्यठ कृष्ण महाराज बेहनोवमय!

Meaning: I have ordered a 'rath' for Devaki, the mother. She has to go to our parents' home to invite them to attend the marriage. I have consulted Nachhpatrika for choosing an auspicious day for the same. I have ordered a rath for the lady who is like Devaki, the loving mother of Lord Krishna. I have brought the rath from the king, decorated it exceedingly and made my son, who is like Lord Krishna to me, sit on it. It was all done according to Nakshatrapatrika.

Manzi Vanvun

मॉन्ज़े रॉच़य सोम्बुरिथ बऽच़ॅय
वॉच़य गंग जमुना सारस्वत,
वासुदीव राज़नि सोम्बरिथ बऽच़ॅय
कृष्णनि मॉन्ज़े राचूय क्युथ,
तुलमुलि अंदरॅय राग्यन्या वॉच़य
वॉच़य गंग जमना सारस्वत,
दीवता बागस तुलमुलि नागस
नागस मंज़ खोत मान्ज़े पोष।

Meaning: All kith and kin have been gathered. Ganga, Yamuna and Saraswati rivers have arrived. King Vasudev's family members have all been collected to attend the 'mehandi raat' of Lord Krishna. Goddess Ragyna arrived from Tulmula. The henna flower has grown in the pond of Tulmul which is the garden of Gods.

Kroor Vanvun

The tradition of drawing flowers and leaves on the walls is very old in India. In Kashmir, ladies sit on the ground near the main door and sing folk songs. The ladies use seven colours in their drawings and the round lot of saffron is put in the center. This drawing is done by the paternal aunt.

सिरिसन्ज़ सथ रंग अथ द्वारस खारिमय
रुति सातु कोंग ट्योक अथ कोरमय।

Meaning: I have drawn flowers and leaves with seven colours on the main door and on the auspicious day, put the round saffron dot in the centre.

Shran Vanvun

In Kashmiri language, its synonyms are vuz-shran or gaud shran, which means energetic bath or dripping of water on an idol. The boy or the girl is made to sit on a platform. Four small girls hold the four corners of the white thin cloth and spread it over his/her head. The vedic mantras are changed, after which he or she proceeds for the bath with milk and water. He/she is made to wear new clothes and sit near the altar of the yagya to give offerings.

अरनि मामनि थवुय पोष वुज़ लिविथ
कृष्ण महाराज़स छु कन्येश्रान

Meaning: Maternal aunt has decorated the place for bathing. Shri Krishna has to take the beautifying bath.

Devgun Vanvun

Devgun is originated from 'devagaman' in Sanskrit, which means the arrival of God. It is held one day before marriage or Yagnopavit.

On this day, vedic yagya is held. After the bath, the bride, bridegroom or the lad (in case of Yagnopavit), proceeds for the offerings near the yagya. This ceremony is called 'Devgun'.

पूरे खोतको सूर्यादिशो दूरे करयो नमस्कार

Meaning: You are looking like the sun, risen from the East in this dress. I salute you from a distance, Brahmachari (i.e. religious student of serving celibacy).

Agnikund Vanvun

A huge altar is prepared with bricks, which are pasted with clay. The priest and the boy for yagnopavit sit around it. Fire is lighted for one night and a day. Offerings of dry fruits, flowers and ghee are made.

अंगनै कोण्डस सोनसंज सेरे
ज़ेरे-ज़ेरे खोरमय अगनय कोण्ड

Meaning: I have used bricks of gold for raising the platform, for lightening the fire for yagnopavit.

Yagnopavit Vanvun

In Yagnopavit ceremony, the main function is garlanding a child with the thread called 'janeu' in Hindi, which is made of cotton thread. The significance is that after this, the boy becomes a Brahmin. The women get emotionally lost in singing the rhymes for this.

सुमन कपसा ववनय आई
कृष्ण जुवने यछ़ाये

Meaning: The cotton plant (out of which, the sacred thread was made) was sown with pious, benevolent mind as was desired by Lord Krishna.

The boy acts as a bhikshak (beggar) and begs for the sake of the family priest. It is called 'abhed', which in Sanskrit means without any feeling of difference. This collection serves as the livelihood for the priest and for his study purposes. The priest persuades the next generations to follow suit.

At the end of the religious function, there is a folk dance.

Marriage Vanvun

On the marriage ceremony of the boy and the girl, house cleaning and invitation ceremonies are held in the same way in the case of Yagnopavit. But other ceremonies differ and their subject of vanvun changes according to the occasions.

(*a*) Masmuchravun (hair opening of the marriageable girl)
(*b*) Manzirath (henna dye)
(*c*) Devgun
(*d*) Lagan (Kanyadaan)

Mehandiraat and devgun ceremonies are performed at the time of marriage. But the subject of mantras as well as vanvun pertains to the marrying boy or the girl.

It is necessary to sing Vanvun on Devgun, which follows mehandiraat. It provides assistance to the celebration through human sensation and expression of doubt and feelings on the occasion as the girl has to go to strangers' house. Among Kashmiri Hindus, at the time of vedic yagya (devgun), red cotton thread is put in the hole of the ears of the girl to hang the hexagon-shaped gold ornament, which is called 'dejhor' in Kashmiri language. In Vedic language, it is called 'aditya-hora'. It indicates lucky future of the girl.

डेजहोर गोरूमय ब्यज ब्रारे
डेक बऽड़ कूरी डेक पूशनय

Meaning: Dejhor was made in Vijeshwara. May she be blessed.

Then comes the turn of 'dwara-puja' (prayer at the door). The bridegroom and the bride stand at the door. Vedic chantings follow. The father of the girl welcomes the father of the boy by saying 'swagatam bhava' (I welcome you). The father of the boy answers 'suswagatam' (I also welcome you). This enchanting moment is accompanied by a vanvun.

भीष्मक राज़नि रोखमि कोमारे
वसदीव राज़नि सालेग्रामस।

Meaning: Today, for the wedding of Rukmini, the daughter of Bhishmak, i.e. Srikrishna, the dear darling of Vasudeva has arrived.

It is followed by the marriage ceremony.

In almost all other Hindu communities, bride and bridegroom touch the feet of their parents after the marriage ceremony to get the blessings. In Kashmir the bride and the bridegroom are worshipped as Shiv and Parvati at the end of the marriage ceremony. The custom is that the bride and the bridegroom are made to sit facing each other and a shawl or preferably a red coloured cloth is spread over them. All the family members and the relatives sprinkle flowers on them. This is called 'posh puja' or the worship with flowers on them.

धर्मराज़ वथुमुत छुस धर्मदानस
गंगा सागर ह्यथ छसव्यतस्ता
छेमू शिव शक्ति पोषि पूजा

Meaning: Dharamraja has arrived with religious values of 'Dharam' along with Ganga Sagar and Vitasta to worship Shiva and Shakti. Today Shiva and Shakti are worshipped as a pair.

Muslim Vanvun

Muslims do not follow the practice of singing vanvun in the same fashion as the Hindus in Kashmir do. Their pattern of singing is different. They divide themselves into two groups. One group sings a line, which is repeated by the other.

At the end of second half of the fourteenth century, Kashmiri Hindu civilization underwent a drastic change. The culture and tradition got a jolt. Vanvun was no exception. Muslims changed the subject and the style of their vanvun from the original.

They sing in fast speed and sometimes get even faster. They do not have that consistency, which Hindus have in vanvun singing. They generally sing standing. Muslims form two groups, facing each other. One group consists of two rows. First row consists of elderly women. The second row keeps standing and the first row holds each other's back. The second row comes forward with one foot and goes back with the other singing vanvun. This type of singing is prevalent in Kumaon and Garhwal hills. The style and the way of tying a printed scarf around their heads is also prevalent there as is prevalent among Muslim women of Kashmir.

मोटर कारस कुन्जकर खोचये
लाले पकनऽवितोन लोत लोतये

Meaning: Have control over the key of the car and drive the same slowly to his in-law's house.

At the time of birth, Muslims celebrate 'shadiana' to bless the child. The newly born child is taken for bath. Through the left ear, 'azaan' and through the right, 'tak baar' is read. 'Azaan' implies welcome to the child and 'Takbaar' reminds the child of the inevitable death.

थनु यलि प्योहम हमदाह पोरमय,
कननूय कोरमय दीनि इस्लाम।

Kashmiri Muslims hold 'Zarkasy' (originated from jata-nishkaran, in Sanskrit) in Kashmir. Seventy five percent Muslims in Kashmir are converted Hindus, which is why, some functions are common. Muslims remove the hair of the boy or the girl child after a year and a half of the birth.

रुत दोह वुछिथ ज़र हो कासय,
उमर ज़ीठ थविनय बोड खोदाय।

Meaning: I have sought auspicious day for your hair removal. May God bless you with long life.

The most important celebration among Muslims is circumcision. They arrange feasts and after the religious ceremony sing vanvun. Among Muslims, vanvun, sung during marriages, comprises of:

(*a*) Tomul-cchattun (rice cleaning)
(*b*) Mehandiraat (henna dye)
(*c*) Masmucchravun (opening of the hair of the girl before marriage)
(*d*) Yenivol (arrival of the groom and the guests)

At the reception of barat, ladies sing vanvun with great enthusiasm.

कुकिली रव त्राव मन्ज़ पोषि वनुनुय
महाराजु मदुन आव लोलो।

Meaning: Nightingale, you sing enchantingly in the center of the flowery garden. The bridegroom is arriving.

It will be right to say that nature provided its charm, delicacy and human touch to the music of Kashmir.

Unfortunately, these days, some absurd contents are being added to Hindu vanvun like, 'the bridegroom arrived late' or 'our girl is educated', etc. Such meaningless additions have brought down the value of vanvun. Thus, Hindu, Vanvun is deviating from its purpose and religious fervour. We have to save it and revive its grace.

Veegya Vacchan

'Veegya vacchan' has originated from a vedic word, 'vishesh yog vacchan', i.e. to be sung on a special occasion. It is sung by Kashmiri Hindu women at the time of Yagnopavit ceremony or at the time of marriage ceremony. When the bridegroom leaves for wedding along with the wedding guests, a round shaped drawing of various designs, in seven colours, is prepared on the white washed piece of ground in the courtyard. It is called 'vyug' in Kashmiri and after the completion of yagnopavit, the boy is made to stand on this and is fed with sweets, after which he is taken to the river for a bath and evening prayers. At his departure, the women of the house stand in a circle, make the lady of the house stand in the center and revolve around her, drawing and singing.

हुम वोथुम वीगि खोतुम
तोत वोथुम यारबल
माम लालनि कौछि खोतुम
तोत वोथुम यारबल।

Meaning: After performing yagya with vedic mantras, the lad has departed to the banks of the river for the bath, after the religious observance. He has been carried by his maternal uncle.

The lady of the house (supposed to be the mother of the boy) dances and sings:

दितुम दयन रोछुम नानि
मे देदि कानि सेयदेयनम

Meaning: God bestowed me with the son. He has been brought up by his grand mother. By holding the lad in my lap, my ribs are tired so much so, that they are almost broken, but now thank God, they are in order again.

The dance movement and singing continues till the women feel that the bath of the lad on the banks of the river is over. They then start the next series:

अस्य करव अरनिव्रत तं ब्ययि वनवुनये
हऽर द्रायि नचेने त सुति सोन संज़िये
अस्य करव अरनिव्रत बेयि वनवुनये
हारि गछ़ि डेजहोर सुति सोनसुन्दये

Meaning: We will sing arnivrat and vanvun. Sharika, the lady, has come down to dance—a golden dance. Sharika should have a dejihor (aditya) to wear.

When the boy leaves for the wedding, the same custom is allowed. Then mother, sister(s) and other women sing:

नचान नचान फलिमा खौर
मे गछ़ि जोर आसुनये
बेनि छु बोय सथा कत्था
मे गछ़ि जोर आसुनये

Meaning: Constant dance has bruised my feet. I should get a gift of a dress. A sister has great expectations from a brother, so I should have a new dress.

Ruf

'Ruf' is a very interesting and emotional type of folk dance. It is called 'Row', in the capital and 'Ruf' in villages. It is directly related with spring. On the basis of the climatic conditions, there are four seasons in Kashmir. Every season lasts for three months. At the outset of spring, Kashmiris entertain themselves by dancing and singing. This practice was prevalent even in the ancient times, which is mentioned in Nilmatapurana. It has been proved that 'Ruf' has been inspired by the bee and is the imitation of the lovemaking of the black bee. 'Ruf' might have been originated from 'dwarf dance', of vedic language. In Vedic language, it means a bee, which further developed as Ruf. In spring, autumn seasons, the black bee comes near the bud but does not touch it, as it seems too shy. It revolves around the bud for a long time, creates a romantic mood by moving back and coming forward again and again. At last, the bud yields and accepts the offer. This movement of the bee might have led to the creation of 'Ruf'.

In 'Ruf' beautiful ladies form two or four groups, consisting of three or four girls. They face each other. Each girl puts her arms on the arms of the other girl. All the girls jointly bring their feet forward and then backward. This is how the dance proceeds. The songs are in question answer form.

In Kashmir, in far-flung villages, usually two groups are formed. One group questions and the other answers, musically, while dancing 'Ruf'.

प्रश्न : पोषि वारि भोम्भुर आव?

उत्तर : रोफ वेरि करने

प्रश्न : पोषि वारि भेम्भुर आव?

उत्तर : रोफ वेरि करने..........
प्रश्न : पोषि मालि अछु मुबुराव?
उत्तर : रोफ वेरि करने...........
प्रश्न : पोषि लंजि असुन त्रोव?
उत्तर : रोफ वेरि करने........
प्रश्न : येम्बरज़लि काड़ त्रोव?
उत्तर : रोफ वेरि करने...........
प्रश्न : त्रायि त्रायि भेम्भुर आव?
उत्तर : रोफ वेरि करने............

Meaning:

Q. : In the garden of flowers, did the black bee arrive?
Ans.: It has come to perform 'Ruf' dance.
Q. : Did the flower open its eyes?
Ans.: It opens its eyes to perform 'Ruf' dance.
Q. : Did the flowery branch, full of blossoms, smile?
Ans.: The bee has come to perform 'Ruf' dance.
Q. : Did the flower yawn and stretch its limbs?
Ans.: The bee has come to perform 'Ruf' dance.
Q. : Did the bee arrive slowly and consciously?
Ans.: It has come to perform 'Ruf' dance.

About fifty years ago, there was a custom among Kashmiri Hindus, Manzirath (one day before marriage, when henna was applied on the bride or bridegroom's hands), Lalleshwari's vakhs were sung in question answer form in the 'Ruf'.

प्रश्न : कुस हा मालि लूसुय न पकान पकान?
उत्तर : जल हा मालि लूसुय न पकान पकान
प्रश्न : कुस हा मालि लूसुय न करान निन्दा?
उत्तर : मनुष्य लूसुय न करान निन्दा

Meaning:

Q. : O dear, who does not get tired, even after continuous walking?

Ans. : O friend, water is not tired of continuous flowing.

Q. : O dear, who is not tired, even after continuous scandalizing?

Ans. : O friend, man does not get tired of scandalizing.

Another example of question answer form used in 'Ruf' is given here. Women show their beauty and youth in colourful dresses and sing:

प्रश्न : बालपानस क्या गच्छि़ आसुन?
उत्तर : बालपानस यावुन छ छावुन
प्रश्न : मेछर यावनुक कति गंछि हावुन?
उत्तर : बोम्बरस सऽत्य मेछर छु छावुन

Meaning:

Q. : What is needed in maidenhood?
Ans. : In maidenhood, youth is to be enjoyed.
Q. : Where is the sweetness of youth to be shown?
Ans. : Sweetness is to be enjoyed with the bee.

Muslims have their separate type of 'Ruf' dance, which they display on their Islamic festivals.

ईद आई रस रस
ईदगाह वसंऽय
ईदगाह वसंऽय

Meaning: My friend, Id has come, Let us go at a slow pace to the Idgah.

The tradition of dancing and singing has been an ancient practice in Kashmir.

Nilamatapurana has mentioned it at several places.

उत्सवं च सदा कार्य गीत नृत्य समाकुलं

Meaning: This public entertaining festival should be organized with dances, sweet songs and musical instruments.

'Ruf' is a continuation of the tradition, indicated in the above line.

Hikat

'Hikat' is an inseparable part of 'raas'. We can even call it a form. Reference to 'raas', prevalent in Kashmir, is available in Bhatt Avatar. Even his predecessor, Nund Rishi, was acquainted with 'raas', originated from 'hi-krit', i.e. any piece of work done joyfully.

In this dance, two girls stand in a circle in pairs facing each other with bright sticks in each hand and strike at each other's stick and sing:

सभिव करव अथयवास,
पकिव रास गिन्दने

Meaning: Let us get together and dance 'raas'.

While striking, the speed of the singing gets faster, after which the girls throw the sticks and one girl holds the right hand of the other girl and the left with the right. The girls then drag the weight of the body towards their backs, touching the fingers of the feet of the girl opposite, with hers. They start moving in a spherical manner to the slow music. Soon, the speed of the movement of the body as well as of the music gets faster. Again, the speed gets slower and the girls lift the sticks and start striking and singing simultaneously.

पकिवी सखियव अऽस्य करव रास लाल बन्धा गिन्दने
हतैय सखियव अऽस्य करव रास लाल बन्धा गिन्दने

Meaning: Come friends, we will hold 'raas' dance and play 'lal bandha' game.

There is another form of 'hikat' that is hikachi, which is performed by small girls. 'Ch', in Kashmiri language, denotes feminine gender. Hikachi gavun is a song, which is sung by small girls, while playing the hikat. This game can be played on any occasion, season or festival.

Two girls hold each other's hands in the form of a cross. The game begins with question answers:

प्रश्न : वोथू बुड्ढा
उत्तर : ब न बोथाई न
प्रश्न : सोन सेन्ज़ वऽज हा दिमव
उत्तर : ब न वोथाई न

Meaning:

Q. : Oldman stand up
Ans.: I will not.
Q. : I will give you gold ring?
Ans.: I will not.

At the end of long dialogues of this type, the girls hold the balance of their bodies backwards, touch each other's feet and sing.

'Hikat' is common among Hindu and Muslim girls. Though 'hikat' songs are not available in large numbers, yet they hold great significance. They do not have any systematic ideas, yet some of them are full of seriousness of the theme.

For example, the following song beautifully presents the future imagination of a girl, in her early teens:

हिक्कटा-मिक्टा, हिक्कटा-मिक्टा,
बऽय अनिनम डूनि काह
हशि-नौशि दिमय क्या
बानकुठि थवं क्या
पानस क्षमं क्या
दोह पॉशि लोकचार
हक्कची चीं।

Meaning: These lines reflect the romantic feelings of the girl about the future. She will be in her in-laws, home. Her brother would come to meet her with almonds. They would be eleven in number. Will the almonds be sufficient for distributing, eating by her mother-in-law and herself? Some are also to be stored. Innocent dreams of the girl have been vividly depicted in these lines. The girl does not seem to have shed her childhood innocence.

Vaan

Vaan is a market or shop in Kashmiri language. Kalhana has used the word 'patvan' in his Raj Tarangini, i.e. market of cloth. In Kashmiri, the actual word for it is 'Vedan', which means crime market. It is popularly known as van in short form. According to Hindu religion, a man goes through sixteen rituals and 'antyeshthi sanskar' is the last among these. In Rig-Veda, ample reference to the expression of grief, made at the time of death, is available. In Indian culture grief songs are in practice even since ancient times. This tradition was prevalent in civilized castes. Unfortunately, it is on the decline.

In Kashmiri Hindus, whenever an old man or woman died, these types of grief songs were performed, i.e. vaan singing was done. Among Kashmiris, grief remains for ten days. In olden days, an old professional singer, who was called 'vangarinya' in Kashmiri, came on the day of the death, enquired about the names of the ancestors and family members etc. and sang till the tenth day. Her body and throat used to choke with grief. The subject of the songs were in praise of the dead and his future in Heaven.

काक गव पानय स्वरगय अन्दर
नौशि कोरि अनेनैय क्या सौन्दर
लरि जायि लज़नय क्या सौन्दर
वेदः परिनय क्या सौन्दर
समय बितोवनय क्या सौन्दर
यूगा सौधनैय क्या सौन्दर

Meaning: The dead person entered the Heaven himself. He got his beautiful daughters married, brought talented daughters-in-law home, built nice houses and did studies of Vedas nicely, spent whole life well and did Yoga, meditation.

Lalnavun

This is a type of folk song, which is sung to make the baby fall asleep. In Hindi, it is called 'Lori', in English, it is called 'Lullaby' and in Kashmiri, it is called 'Lalnavun'. 'Lalnavun' is based on Vatsalaya Ras. It reflects motherly love, which is pure. It depicts the unbroken bond between the mother and the child. Usually, Ram, Krishna, Yashodhra and Kaushalaya are the main subjects of Lalnavun.

लाला लुलि मन्ज़ ललनावय।
गूर हो करय कनदूर गरय।।

माल हो करय गुलि जाफरे।
गूर हो करय कनदूर गरय।।

साल हो करय गुलि जाफरे।
गूर हो करय कनदूर गरय।।

प्याल हो बरय गुलि जाफरे।
गूर हो करय कनदूर गरय।।

चन्दन हो गरय गुलि जाफरे।
गूर हो करय कनदूर गरय।।

Meaning: O child, I will swing you in my lap and prepare ear ornaments for you. O my flower of marigold, I will make a garland for you, I will host a party for you and make 'moun' for you.

सोन्दुरोबि सौन सन्दल गरय
हो-हो करय शाम सौन्दरय
जस दा क्या अस बागिवान
यस युथ टोठैव सन्तान
कौशल्या क्या अस बागिवान
यस युथ टोठैव सन्तान।

Meaning: In the above mentioned song, the child is imagined like Krishna and Ram and their mothers are like

Yashodhra and Kaushalya. In Lalnavun songs, the mother prays for the long life of the child. These songs depict the mother's fondness and love for the child. The main idea behind these Lalnavun songs is to make the child sleep.

In the book, 'Thirty songs from the Punjab and Kashmir', Ratan Devi Coomaraswamy writes about the cradle songs of the Kashmiri Lullabies. "The cradle songs are perfect in their own way; unlike so many so called lullabies in modern music. They could scarcely be simpler; the beautiful vowel sounds, tune and rhythm combine to form a true croon".

SONGS SUNG BY MINSTRELS

These types of songs are those, which are sung by the professionals from the point of view of earning money. In this category fall the songs sung by the Chhakar singers, bhands and ladishah singers and more.

Bhand Paethar

Singing and dancing by bhands has contributed a lot to the traditional music of Kashmir from the ancient period. Not only in Kashmir, but also in other places, bhand paethar (custom) has remained prevalent from the very ancient period.

In Kashmir, existence of bhands has remained very popular. Nilmatapurana tells us that bhand paethar was very famous in Kashmir and bhands performed during festivals and other occasions. In Nilamatapurana, the word 'mandavanam' is mentioned, which means dance and songs by the bhands.

'Bhand' comes from 'bhaana' a satirical and realistic drama, generally a monologue that is mentioned in Bharata's Natyashastra. The Bhand Paether is not a monologue but a social drama, incorporating mythological legends and contemporary social satire. Born Hindus, the bhands converted to Islam and remain very secular in their outlook.

The Bhand has to train himself, to be a skillful actor, dancer, acrobat and musician. The leader of the troupe is called 'the magun', a word taken from 'mahagun', a man of varied talents. He teaches his pupil the art and expertise of their inheritance. Today, the training is non-existent.

The bhands dance to the tune of a specified 'mukam' and the orchestra includes the shahnai, dhol, nagara and the thalij. Before the Swarnai player adopts his newly made instrument, a ritual offering is made in a 'dargah'.

The composition played is called a 'mukam' and each bhand paether has its own. The music follows a set pattern—the salaam, thurav, duitch, nav patti and the salgah. There is a highly developed system of music based on the classical mould, the Sufiana Kalaam with intricate and codified patterns.

The man who plays the dhol is the central figure in the orchestra. Many tools, in various combinations, are played on this drum but today very few remain. The nagara is an accompaniment to the dhol and the rhythm doubles in intensity as the playing proceeds. More than one nagara is used in the performance to emphasize the sound of the instrument. The thalij is a metal cymbal, a little larger than those used in other musical forms. To this music, are added Kashmiri folk songs, which are sung throughout the play.

The properties that are a must for every paether are a whip and a short bamboo stick. The 'koodar' or the long whip as crafted from the dry stem of the 'bhang' plant and looks like a thick rope, which is forked at its tip. When used, it emanates a sound similar to gunshot. During the performance, a character can be whipped a hundred times, without being hurt, because this property does not have the impact associated with the whip; it just looks deadly. It is used to transform all the elements that represent oppression into strong dramatic images. In sharp contrast, the 'bans' are used by the jester or 'maskhara'. These are split bamboo sticks that make a sharp sound.

Besides these, 'kaper chadar' or sheet of cloth is also used as a curtain. Some of the actors make their entry from behind this curtain.

With time, the music has changed and unfortunately, the traditional 'mukam ragas' are not played as much.

राज लेफितल चाव बेखबर गछ़िथ
वजीर छि दौयि अथु दऽर प्राटान
लूठ गव गामस लुटऽरि गयि चलिथ
शे मन लेफितल राज ख्रोखमारान

Meaning: The king is unmindfully sleeping under the quilt. The villages have been ransacked and the king is sleeping peacefully under the six feet long quilt.

A new direction has been made in the Kashmiri bhand paether and the credit goes to Shri M. L. Kemmu.

Ladishah

'Ladishah' is originated from ladi and Shah. 'Ladi' means a row or line—'Shah' has been added with the passage of time with the coming of Muslim rulers.

'Ladishah' is a satirical song, which reflects the society's condition. It is a type of song, which makes people laugh, but at the same time, it is a satire on the existing government.

The singers of 'ladishah' remain in groups and carry an instrument with them, which is called 'dhukar' or 'dhukru'. 'Dhukar' is made of iron (1 -1.5 mtrs. long), with metal rings hanging around it. The singers wander from village to village. They generally go to other villages at the time of harvest to earn their livelihood.

They are satirists, who compose their songs on the spot, on the issues pertaining to social, small and big evils. Their manner is very humorous and entertaining, but bitter at the same time.

In the history of Kashmir, there was a king named 'Mukunda'. His ears were very big. Thus, he wore a huge turban to hide them. This secret was only known to his barber. Unfortunately, the barber died. As a result, the king engaged a new one and directed him to hide the secret of his big ears. He never knew that the new barber was a 'ladishah'. The barber disobeyed the king and the secret was exposed to the public like this:

मॉकन राजस मॉशिहुन्द कन
कन छि यीत्याह यूताह वन
मॉकन राजस मॉशिहुन्द कन

Meaning: King Mukund's ears are of the size of the ears of a buffalo. Ears are as big as a huge forest.

Similarly, when the aeroplane came to Kashmir, satirical verses were composed.

हवाई जहाज आव मुल्कि कश्मीर
यिमव वुछ तिमव कोर तौब तख्सीर
जमालस कमालस नस कम्य वट
यिमव वुछ तिमव कोर तौब तख्सीर
जूनि वोन राजस तुफान छु ईरान
यिमव वुछ तिमव कोर तौब तख्सीर
गाऽन्ठ हिश नभय प्यंठ ग्रायि मारान
यिमव वुछ तिमव कोर तौब तख्सीर
शोर छुस यूताह जन कन चीरान
यिमव वुछ तिमव कोर तौब तख्सीर

Meaning: The aeroplane comes to Kashmir for the first time. Anyone who saw it made a hue and cry. Nothing bad was done by Jamal and Kammal who came out to see the aeroplane, because everyone came out from the house to see it. Whoever saw it, made a hue and cry. The plane went circular like an eagle. Whoever saw it, made a hue and cry. Much noise was created by the plane and the ears got hurt by the noise. Whoever saw it, made a hue and cry about it.

Chhakar

'Chhakar' has an important place in the Kashmiri folk music tradition. It entertains old and young ladies and gents. It may be the originated form Rigvedic 'Shaktri' or anti-shakri rhyme. In Aryan culture, chorus singing after deva-yagya was a common practice. But according Shri Mohan Lal Aima, 'mantrya manḍ's ghada instrument originated 'chhakri'. Ghada, has an important place in 'chhakri'. Tumbaknari is another compulsory instrument in 'chhakri', which is a kind of long gourd. It is open from the back. On the front side of the tumbaknari, the skin of a cat is stuck. Usually, ghada is played by men and tumbaknari by women. Sometimes, sarangi and rabab are also the accompaniments. Male dancers perform dance, which is called 'back-kot' (originated from Vedic vatkat.) 'Chhakri' has great relationship with farmers, who at a break from the hard task, sing and dance in the evenings. 'Yagnopavit' and marriage ceremonies are not possible without 'Chhakri'. On an auspicious day, tumbaknaris are purchased and 'Chhakri' singing begins from the house cleaning ceremony.

The credit of making 'Chhakar' famous in Kashmir, goes to the professional artists who, along with their full team, sing and create a musical environment, which is full of fun and entertainment. 'Chhakar' traditionally was confined to villages, though songs, set to 'Chhakri' music, were sung on wedding occasions in the urban areas. The credit of popularizing it goes to Radio Kashmir. We often watch 'Chhakar' programmes on T.V. or hear it on All India Radio, in the valley.

Chhakar' gayaki is not new. This type of folk song has been in practice for a long time. According to Raj Tarangini, king Bhashmakar had made a type of folk song popular in which, utensils of clay or brass were used. Even today, we find gaagar, chimta, matka, ghada, etc. being used as the instruments with 'Chhakar' gayaki.

'Chhakar' is sung collectively in a group. 'Chhakar', which is sung by professionals, has only men in it. A very important feature of 'Chhakar' gayaki is that the singers themselves play the instruments. The style of singing is such that the first line of the song is sung by the leading singer. The same line is repeated by other members of the group. The speed of the song gets very fast and the words get difficult to understand. When 'Chhakar' is in its full swing, people from around get up and start dancing.

Undoubtedly, it is a very popular and entertaining folk song.

लाला लगयो बाल बावस
राम नावस पार्य लगय

Meaning : O lad, I will sacrifice myself for your child like actions and get lost in your name, Ram.

कत्यू छुक नुन्द बाने
वलो माशोक म्योन
शराबन्य प्याल बरयो
गोलाबन माल करयो
पगाह या कऽल्य ब मरयो
वलो माशूक म्याने

Meaning : The maiden is separated from her lover and remembers him. "Where are you my lover? Please come to me. I have filled the cups with wine and made rose garlands for you. Come, O my lover or else I will die in a day or two".

Bachhi Nagma

The general meaning of the 'bachhi nagma' is adolescent melodious voice. But in villages, it is still known by the old name 'bachhi gyavun'. During Pathan reign (1757-1818), the Arabic word 'nagma' must have been added to it. So it is the mixture of 'bachhi' (originating from sanskrit) and 'nagma' (originating from Arabic). The dress of the dancer is round and very loose and long, upto the feet. Upto the waist, it is tight. 'Ghunghroos' are tied to the lower side of the legs. Sometimes they keep long hair. This dress matches the dress of a 'Kathak' dancer. Such dances are very old in India. This has been mentioned in Nilamatapurana.

The Kashmiris have great liking for the dance and music of 'bachha nagma'.

The dancing boys are professional singers. They are booked in advance for marriages, yagnopavit of other functions. The troupe consists of six or seven members— One, a leading singer and others, the prayers of rabab, sarang, etc. An atmosphere of entertainment is created by singing, the sound of payals, the trembling and wavering movements, the actions of both hands, the tender singing voice, by their holding the corners of long vesture from right and left side and by variety, in expressions. Slow and melodious modulation of music reminds of the rhythm of flowing water-falls.

हारि शोगस छि लजिमूच मानमान
बोजि व्यसिये बोलान शोगु जान

Meaning : The nightingale and the parrot are in mutual competition. Friend! Listen and scc, the parrot surpasses the nightingale in singing.

Rishi Macchar

'Rishi Macchar' has been originated from the vedic 'Rishi + Mat + har. i.e. insane or intoxicated movements of the Rishis. 'Rishi Macchar' is known as 'Rishi Bechhun' i.e. Rishi's begging. In ancient times, we used to spare some time from meditation once a week and go to other villages to beg for food in the name of God. Whatever they received as alms, was accepted by them.

They were spiritually intoxicated. Ladies of the houses name this known as 'Rishi Macchar'. Kashmir is known a Rishivar, means the abode of Rishis.

Rishi tradition of Kashmir has been mentioned in No. 203 of Mahabharata. Kashyao was also a Rishi. Even Muslims have respect and faith for them. Rishi Macchar Saints used to move in groups, enter the courtyard of any house and repeat those rhymes, which pertained to the morality of life. Kashmiri Hindu and Muslim women used to put questions about the future of their husbands and family.

Here are a ew examples:

ऋषि मोल ज़पान दैय नाव पानय
छि मंगान रॅच़र सारिनुय क्युत

Meaning: Rishis are themselves lost in meditation. They pray happiness for all.

फकीर आंगन च़ामय
तति खैरात मंगानय
खैरात दिमसय पानय
अज़ रोज़ सानि महमानय।।

सतज़न गर म्योन च़ामय
खोर तस छल ब पानय
दक्षिना दिमसय मानय
अज़ रोज़ सानि महमानय।।

Meaning: The saint has come to my country and to receive aims. I will offer myself. You stay over at our place as an honourable guest. I will wash your feet myself.

Dhamaly

'Dhamaly' means leaping and jumping. 'Dhamaly' or 'Dhamali' is a holy sport in Brij in Uttar Pradesh. It is related with an exercise of Saints who jump over burning fire. This word is common in Kashmir. When small children leap and jump, they are directed not to do 'Dhamali', i.e. jumping. This is a dance performed by fifteen to twenty persons. Ladies do not take part in it. The whole team wears white cotton dress and a head gear. Two dholaks are the accompanying instruments. When one gets tired, the other plays. The dance fully depends on the dholak. A little fault spoils the vehicle show. The group stands in a circle. The leader addresses them:

करीव मत्यव अही

Meaning: O mad (companions), give blessings.

They, then, play dholak and dance in 'raas' form and act as if they pray to some divine power for the blessings and sing together:

असि रूत तोहि रूत ज़गतस रूत

Meaning: God may bless us, you and the whole world.

Then one actor comes forward and does 'bhangra' type actions and jumps about two meter high. Others whistle to encourage him. He is called 'Damali Fakir'. He then sings:

दीतवी दीतवी वेष्नार पन
दमाल्य गोसन्य चाव तोहि आंगन

Meaning: You must offer something for the sake of Vishnu. Saints have entered your courtyard.

At times the dancers carry about one meter long stick and strike and counter strike. Their dance resembles 'raas'. All the ladies bring their children to get blessings. This dance is held in spring, when rice is sown. Their second visit begins after summer season, then they go to religious places, grave yards, abodes of peers and fakirs and religious fairs to give a display of their skills.

SONGS SUNG BY FARMERS

Naindai Gyavun

Naindai Gyavun is related to farmers folk songs. Naind is the changed form of the word 'Ninad of Sanskrit'. The word 'gyavun' also has originated from gayan of Sanskrit. India is an agricultural country. The tradition of agricultural songs is prevalent in every state and region. The nature of agricultural songs is joyful exciting and merrymaking. The people in Kashmir are rice eaters. To prepare the paddy fields is not an easy task. It requires hard labour with proper planning. Singing makes difficult tasks of the farmers easy and enhances their zeal. After cultivation, the land becomes uneven and soil lumps are formed. The lumps are broken and the soil is made even. The task of breaking of soil lumps is called 'Yattpur'. After 'Yattpur' farmers sow paddy plants. Sowing of paddy plants is called 'Thal'. When the plants start dancing in the breeze, the farmers come back for cultivation of the soil and weed. Making the fields suitable for agriculture is called 'Naindai'. In harvest season which comes in Kashmir in October and November farmers have to be quick and vigilant in harvesting and carrying grains for storing. They are scared of the uncertainty of rains and snow. They find no breathing time in between, but sometimes give pause to their work. They sit beneath a tree and entertain themselves with singing. It is accompanied by 'Manjira' etc. Since these songs sung in chorus pertain to farming, they are called 'Naindan Chhakar'. Here are certain examples.

They give free flow to the rhythmic tones under the open sky:

तलद्राव ब्योलुय कुल आव बारसस
व्यसि वन्तमि टॉठिस कति प्रारस
कलजीर तिहयीरि दिचफोलवनिस पानस
व्यसि वन्तमि टॉठिस कति प्रारस

अशि ग्रायि सगवोन्य बु वोन्य त्रावस
व्यसि वन्तमि टॉठिस कति प्रारस
लरि लरि ब्योलवोवान बु ब्रोठ द्रायस
व्यसि वन्तमि टॉठिस कति प्रारस
खोर पिशुल डूर छु खूंर सनिराव स
व्यसि वन्तमि टॉठिस कति प्रारस

Meaning: The seeds have sprouted. The plant has gained entity. O my friend you tell how long shall I have to wait for my lover? The top of the plant is giving a jerk to its blooming self. O my friend, how long shall I wait for my lover? I will water this plant with the flow of the tears of my eyes. You tell my how long shall I wait? Lost in the thought, of my lover, I have gone much forward while transplanting in paddy. You tell me how long shall I wait? The fields are slippery with wet soil. I have to press down my foot. How long shall I wait for my lover?

The song shows the throbbing pain of an innocent maiden in separation from her lover. The melodious style of singing makes the pain mild and sober. Her feeling does not disturb her working. In Kashmir, in summer, it is the maidens who go for hoeing and weeding the land for wheat, kidney beans, etc. The weeding instruments, like the khurpi or tongrues are used on low and high land. The work inspires them to sing full throatedly.

वोथि व्येसि चूर दिमव अथ मोंग ड़ारस
यारस याद पैयस ज़न्य छि प्रारान
वोथि व्येसि चूर दिमव अथ मोंग ड़ारस
यारस याद पैयस ज़न्य छि प्रारान
वोथि व्येसि चूर दिमव अथ मोंग ड़ारस
यारस याद पैयस ज़न्य छि प्रारान

Meaning : Get, up, O friend, we will go to the Kidney bean fields for weaning Unwanted plants. May be my darling will be reminded that I am waiting. Get up O friend, we will go to paddy fields for weaning unwanted plants.

The plugging is done at three stages: Firstly, on dry land, then on wet land and then at the time of weeding. When farmers' maiden or newly married daughter-in-law does the job for the first time, her parents, brothers, sisters, uncles and aunts come to help her and all sing in one tone:

बोय ओय बेरे बेरे, थजकादस करी वल्य वल्य,
बायि लयो दुसकिस रादस, थजकादस कर वल्य वल्य

Meaning: The daughter-in-law is addressed. "Your brother is coming along the parapet to help you. Hurry up in transplantation". Her answer is O my brother and I will offer myself a sacrifice for the length of your 'dussa' (a big giant shawl of 5 mtr. Pashmina).

The impact of the forced conversation of Hindus to Islam can be traced from the following two songs sung by Muslims and Hindus.

Muslims sing:

में दज ववुमय करू लोलो
नबी सॉबुन तरू लोलो

Meaning: I have sown the paddy plants. You be merry and go to the graveyard of Nabi Sahab to promise there to offer something after the fulfilment of my desire.

Hindus sing:

में दज ववुमय लोलो करॅ
भैरव सॉहबुन लोलो तरॅ

Meaning: I have sown the paddy plants. You be merry and go to Bhairav temple to promise there to offer something after the fulfilment of my desire.

The occasion of merry making and melodious singing comes when autumn, i.e. season of harvesting begins. Again the girls begin their work of reaping and singing in their melodious voice. We remember the words of words worth in 'The Solitary Reaper' "reaping and singing by herself" in Kashmir, the songs have a tinge of romance.

लोनान लोनान अथ छिम छोकान
डूर छुन मोकलान वनु तय मदनस
चटान चटान अथ आयि श्रोकान
डूर छुन मोकलान वनु तय मदनस
तालिप्यठ गुमदार आयि पशपान
डूर छुन मोकलान वनु तय मदनस
सनु रंग धांकुल ग्रायि मारान दानिकुल
डूर छुन मोकलान वनु तय मदनस।

Meaning: Constant reaping has made my hands tired. Still the field is looking bigger and bigger. Go and tell my lover, harvesting has bruised my hands and still the field looks bigger and bigger. In the heat of autumn season, drops of sweat are coming down from my forehead. The field yet looks bigger, i.e. no end to work is visible. Go and tell my lover.

RELIGIOUS SONGS

Leela

Leela songs are the songs dedicated to God. Prayer songs in Kashmiri were written in Sanskrit in the past which were dedicated to Shiva Shakti, Vishnu and to Baudh Dharam. Kashmir has been the place of Rishis whose every action was consecrated to spiritual powers. We can hear Hindus in temples reciting the couplets from panchastavi (prayer book in Sanskrit) even today.

Reference to the devotional songs in Kashmiri has been made by Ksemendra whose period has been calculated between tenth and twelfth centuries:

"ततः क्षीवो गुरूः कंचित्स्वकांव्यं देषभाषया।"

Meaning : That old 'Guru' selected a devotional poetry book form his native language from his personal library.

The word 'कंचित्स्वकांव्यं' in the above line proves the fact that there were more such poems available at that time. But they were destroyed later by the cruel attacks from outside. Sultan Sikandar was the worst of all. He burnt ancient valuable books on religion, philosophy etc. In the words of Dr. Usha Bagati "इस आक्रान्क होली में अधिकांश लीलापरक काव्यों का विद्वंस हुआ"।

The Book 'Mahanay Prakash' written in Kashmiri by Shrikanth is deemed to have belonged to eighth or ninth century.

अक्क काल अक्क पदि वातो
चोदस्यु पूज नू मार्यादो

Meaning : After the blessings of Guru, meeting with God becomes easy and there is no importance of the ritual of Chaturdashi prayer.

Certain devotional verses of Kashmiri language belonging from tenth to thirteenth century are available. They throw light on 'Pandit Kalaam'.

अक्रयी करमा सूँय अति सारन
अदु चूँही दोरबल सहज़ व्यच़ार

Meaning : To attain oneness with God is possible only by enjoying devotional songs with concentration and by unearthly religious practices.

Next follows the period of Lal Dyad (14th century) popularly known as Lalleshwari whose Vakhs have depth of mysticism.

गगन च़य बूतल च़य
ज़य द्यने पवन त रात।
अरग चंदन पोश पोनि च़य
सोरूय च़य त लागिज़िय क्याह।

Meaning : What should we offer you in worship. You are the sky, you are the earth, you are the air, the day and night, you are the sacrificial grain the sandal paste, you are the flowers, the water and all that exists.

दीव वटा दीव खटा
प्यठ ब्वन, छुय ईक वाठ।
पूज़ कस करख हतो, बटा
कर मनस त पवनस संगार।।

Meaning: The idol is but stone. So is the temple from top to bottom, it is one mass. Whom will you worship, O imprudent Brahmin? Try to join your prana with the mind.

Another poet who created history by his contribution to the devotional music of Kashmir is Nund Rishi.

ल प्रेनिस बदनस मोनुक दाग गोम
ज़ाग गोम नीरिथ बार्गं अन्दुरैय
हारनिस तापस पोह तुँ भाग गोम
फाग गोम नीरिथ हर बिन्दुरैय

Meaning : Old apparel of mine has received a stain. Sentient being has left the garden. Resultantly the warmth of the sunlight of summer season has changed to winter cold weather. I am deprived of the advantages of summer. It is a mystic statement, meaning thereby that the sins I commit have changed the advantages which would have been in my share to disadvantages which are due to a sinner.

At another place, he confesses that he has led a materialistic life to the ignorance of the fact that the world was false and artificial.

ब युथ ज़ान ह दुनिया छु केंह नै,
नाहकु दुनियिहिच बरह नँ ब्रांत।

Meaning: After Nund Rishi, comes the name of Habba

Khatoon, whose singing talent raised her to the height of a queen. Her lines are famous.

च कम्यू सोनि म्यानि भ्रम दिथ न्यून खो।
चे ति क्याज़ि गयो म्यन्य दंय।।

Meaning : Some lady has lured you and you have developed hate for me.

Another famous female singer has been Arnimal in 18th century. This intellectual singer assembled all the old tunes and preserved them in her sentiments. These songs are the precious treasure of traditional songs for Kashmiris.

अरनि रंग गोम श्रावण हिये
कर ई ये दरशुन हिये

Meaning : The sizzling beautiful colour, which nature has in 'Savan' (July) has changed to winter. When will he come to bless me with his presence?

There is hardly any Kashmiri, whose eyes are not filled with tears on listening to the pathetic and melodious renderings of Arnimal.

In Ram Leela and Krishan Leela, Kashmiri poets have contributed abundantly to the religious poetry in Kashmiri Language. Prakash Ramayan, Shankar Ramayan, Anand Ramayan, Vishnu Pratap Ramayan, Amar Ramayan have a distinguished place in Leela tradition. Among Krishna devotees, the poet Parmanand is well known. He went to the village, contacted old women to learn the tradition which they were preserving by singing. He revived the ancient culture and the devotional fervor, which Martand temple once had and which was destroyed by the cruelty of foreign invaders. Parmananda realized that old women had given patronage to it in their homes in villages. He made the most of it.

He revived it with musical tunes and paved the way for the future Leela singers like Laxmanjoo, Bulbul and

Krishanjoo Razdan. He depicted different stages in the life of Lord Krishna, like his childhood and youthful actions with Gopis (married women who flirted with Lord Krishna).

दीवकीय हन्दि परमानन्दो
जशोदा नदनीय श्री गूविंदो
दीवकीय हुन्दि परमानन्दो
वन्दयो दौध पादन कपालो
करयो च़्ये किच पोश मालो
लालो लालो बाल गूपालो

Meaning : O! Source of joy for Devki and the son of Yashoda, I will bow before you and make flower garden for you (The devotee has mentioned his own name 'Parmananda').

After Parmananda, the notable name is that of Krishna Das, who was a composer and a singer of Leelas. Following devotional lines are on everybody's lips:

पादि कमलन तल ब आयसय
करनि चऽनि अस्तुती

Meaning : I have come to worship before your lotus like feet.

The tradition of Kirtan (singing devotional songs in chorus) in temples by males, females as well as children is old in Kashmir. Songs devoted to Ram and Krishan are sung regularly. Anand Ji's poetry pertaining to Ram's childhood is well known:

लाला लगयो बाल भावस
राम नावस पार्य लगय

Meaning : O Ram, I will sacrifice my self for your childhood actions.

Kashmir is known or Shaivism, Amarnath, Harmukh Ganga, Mahadeva are ancient pilgrimages, where devotees go to pay homage. The following lines are devoted to Lord Shiva:

पम्पोशि पादन सूती इतम अस्तय अस्तय
च़रन वन्दय जुव जान वंलिज दस्तय
लोल सूतिय पोन्य वुज़हे नागुराज़स्तय

Meaning: O Shiva, pay visit to me with slow steps with your lotus like feet. I will sacrifice body, mind and all. The dry pond of my love will be filled again, if you come.

The tradition of Leela singing will remain intact. Though Kashmiris have been displaced, their listening to Leela Cassettes and assembling at respective regions and singing Leelas in unison on festivals like Navreh and Sonth (spring festival of Kashmiris).

3

Instruments Used with the Traditional Music of Kashmir

In this chapter, I have written about the instruments which are used with the folk music of Kashmir, followed by the description of those instruments which are used with the Sufiana Mousiqui. The history of the instruments, the technique of playing, and the material they are made of and much more has been discussed in the Chapter.

Raj Tarangini mentions specifically about the art of music and musical instruments in this region in distant past. The ancient musical instruments used in Kashmir had been more or less a reflection of the Indian musical instruments in usage during that time.

According to Pandit Kalhana, the folk musical instruments like earthen pots, brass vessels etc. were used by Kashmiri people from very early times. In Kashmir 4th century A.D. tile, found during excavation from Harwan, is showing the impression of a female musician playing on a drum. The other person is shown playing a veena in an artistic pastime. The king Bhiksacara (1120-21) A.D., who himself played these instruments was fond of "Chhakri" (folk choral singing) which continues to be popular in Kashmir valley since Kalhana's time and even earlier to that.

Raj Tarangini mentions an instrument called

"Hadukka" which can be compared to a big pipe.

According to B.C. Deva, the string instruments, Rabab and Sarangi, came to Kashmir with the influence of Muslims. The whole subcontinent was affected by the culture of the new rulers. In music, we came across new Ragas, new styles and new instruments like Rabab and Sarangi. Rabab traveled with the bards and minstrels of Afghanistan and joined the folk group instruments in Kashmir. Some scholars say that it must have been introduced into Kashmir at the time of Zain-ul-Abidin. The most popular instrument used in folk music is the Rabab, which was borrowed from Persia.

Both the instruments, Rabab and Sarangi, used in folk music 'Chhakri' from 14th century onwards opened a new chapter in Kashmir for music and its musical instruments. According to V.N. Bhatkhande, the Muslim rulers had brought with them their own system of music with new melodies, new interpretations, new types of songs and new Talas, which in course of time got fused with Hindu music and gave rise to modern Hindustani music. In a similar way, artists from Central Asia, during Sultanate period, brought with them their art, music, musical instruments and culture resulting in wonderful interaction which in course of time gave birth to Kashmiri classical music which is known as Sufiana Mosiqui. It borrowed its style from Persian music. The cultural interaction has resulted in a unique form and an interesting synthesis of the various types of classical music preserved by Kashmir. It was in this period that the Kashmiri music reached the heights of perfection under the patronage of rulers and saints. Many improvements were brought out in the conventional instruments to render them more useful to the art. The instruments like Santoor, Saaz, Setar, Rabab and Sarangi are resultant inventions and innovations and denote the developments, which took place during this period.

The musical instruments have played a key role in

the evolution of Kashmiri Sufiana Mosiqui. This mosiqui has deep impression on the listener and it is in the nature of very serious music. The Kalam or the verses are also peculiar and this style of music has been very selective in this respect. Similar is the case of instruments used in this Mousiqui, which have been selected with due thought. The instruments used by the sufiana musicians are quite different from those used in Indian Classical Music, Kashmiri folk music and other styles. The prominent instruments include Santoor, Kashmiri Setar (Sehtar) and Saaz-i-Kashmir, the percussion instrument for providing rhythmic variety is Tabla which replaced/Wasul or a Dolke called Dokra, used previously.

Tumbaknari

Tumbak has been a musical instrument in the good olden days in Iran and Central Asia, which was being played mostly by the women folk of these places. Many authors believe that such instrument is being used in Iran and Arabia too. May be it has come to Kashmir from these places, for the simple reason that visitors and rulers were coming to Kashmir in the olden days from Iran and middle east, which besides other things made cultural invasion on the art of Kashmir. Co-incidently, this instrument is also being played by the women folk in Kashmir, the only difference is that in Iran or Central Asia, it is now being made of wood, while in Kashmir, it is still being made of baked clay maintaining its originality. This type of instrument is used for keeping rhythm and also time that covers in a performance of music.

Dr. Rahullah-Khaliqui has written in page no. 403 of his book 'Serguzashti Mousiqui-Iran' about the style of playing this instrument in Iran. In Iran, this instrument is called Tumbakh or Tunbak. In west, it is tumbal or tumbari and in Kashmir, it is tumbaknaeer. The naer is added because the tail end of this instrument is like a pipe, which in Kashmiri, is called a Nore, which has in course of time, changed to naer, making the instrumental tumbaknaer. It is generally used by women folk at various occasions of merriment like marriages, Yagnopavit etc. It is struck by the fingertips to produce the desired harmonious rhythm.

Thalez: is used at farms especially on weeding of paddy crops, when rice plants are required to be freed of the unnecessary growth of vegetation. At these weeding operations, the farmers and their women folk used to sing collectively to overcome the monotonous work, using Thalej as rhythm maintainer.

Sarang (Sarangi)

It is a stringed musical instrument played with a bow and it is in vogue in three types:

- The first type is smaller in size and is used in Kashmir under the name of Sarang, which as per a belief (local) is the invention of Maharaja Sarang Dev's time (Sarang Dev was a king of Kashmir).
- The second type is slightly bigger in size than the Kashmiri Sarang and is mostly used in Bengal for Bengali music.
- The third type is a full size and standard Sarangi used in Indian classical music. Its size is roughly three feet long and about eight inches wide. It has four main strings and about thirty five sympathetic side strings known as Taraba in musical language and most of them are made of steel and brass.

Kashmiri Sarang

Kashmiri Sarang is very simple in structure. It is made of a block of wood, preferably of mulberry or teakwood. The entire body is hollow from inside with two combined parts. Both the sides of the lower part are punched and the whole is covered with hide. The upper part serves the purpose of a fingerboard. Commonly its length is one and a half feet. It has two strings of gut, one of steel and another of coiled brass (making four mains trings). Besides it has eight or ten sympathetic wires/strings of steel known as 'terban'.

It is played with a bow, made of a hard round stick of wood, to which hair of the tail of horse are fixed at both the ends, and a small wooden triangular but curved bridge is placed at one end to keep the hair light. The bow is held in the right hand and moved from one end to the other, vertically on the main strings to produce sound. The fingers namely fore, middle, ring and sometimes the little finger are used to produce notes of different pitch at different length of different strings. The fingers however do not press down the strings on the fingerboard, but are simply touched at the starting place with nails of each finger of the left hand, thus the musical notes are produced.

Besides Kashmir, in the hilly areas of Himachal Pradesh, the playing of this Sarang is common. It is also popular among the tribals of Bihar. In northern India, Sarang, besides being played with the bow-shaped stick, is also played with the 'Kanishtha' (the little finger) and 'anamika' (the finger between the middle and the little finger) of the left hand. The playing on this instrument is known as 'purva'.

Gagar

Gagar is a well known word in the Indian languages. Gagar is made of brass. In Kashmiri Hindu society, Gagar has a cultural importance.

In Kashmir also, at the time of Herath Festival, Gagar has an important role to play. Gagar is placed on the bangle shaped circle made of dry paddy straw which is placed on the floor, washed with clay. The Gagar is half filled with dry nuts. Then Lord Shiva and Shakti are worshipped. Thus, it can clearly be understood that Gagar holds valuable place in the religious festivals in Kashmir. It is also used in homes for storing water by Hindus and Muslims both.

The same Gagar is used with the music of Kashmir. The artist put iron rings in his fingers of the left hand and places his hand on Gagar while striking Gagar with the right hand. The sound produced is very high and thus Gagar plays an important role in creating the musical environment in the gatherings.

During festivals and temple kirtan, playing of Gagar is of great importance. Gagar might have its origin in Vedic time.

Nagada

Nagada is an instrument resembling 'Dhola'. It has many names, like Nakkara, Nagada, Dugdugi etc. in Indian languages. According to B. Chaitanyadeva, Nagada is a changed form of the ancient Dundubhi. In Himachal Pradesh also, its similar form and structure can be found: its upper side is covered with leather of goat. Nagada is slightly smaller than the 'Nobat' instruments. The instrument 'Nagadi' is also played with it. This instrument is struck with a piece of wood and the sound is produced, it is in demand in the temples.

In Kashmir, it is used during festivals and marriage ceremonies. Mainly it is used with the 'bhand jashan' and 'bhand natya'. It is used during paddy harvesting. The farmers consider it as an energy booster during their tiring task of farming.

Dhola

Dhola has its own history in the musical instruments of India. The first form can be traced in the Mohan Jodaro culture. One of the oldest instruments of India, Dhola is mainly traced in the villages and every state of India.

In Kashmir, it is mainly used in villages and it is mostly played with the folk dance of the bhands.

Shankh

One of the ancient instruments of India, Shankh, the sushir-vadya, is associated with religious functions. In Atharva Veda, one finds reference to Shankh, though it existed long before. In Bhagvad Gita, during the time of war, Shankh had played an important role. One finds that Shankh has been called by different names like Panch Janya Shankh, Devadatt Shankh, Mahashan Ponder Shankh and more. Even in Valmiki's Ramayana, the mention of a Shankh can be traced.

In Kashmiri Hindu culture, Shankh is an instrument, which is played both in temples and homes.

In the temples, Shankh is played in the mornings and evenings during the prayers. In homes, it is played before the starting of havan, yagnopavit, marriage, etc. in Kashmiri Hindu marriage, Shankh is played by a person to mark the arrival of the groom. After reaching the bride's place, the groom is made to stand on the 'rangoli' and Shankh is played constantly. At times, when the bride's parents take much time to see her off, then Shankh is played to indicate the late departure, so that they hurry up. Shankh is used as the proclamation and declaration of war, victory and religious ceremonies.

Shankh has a vital role in 'Leela' singing. It gives religious touch to the occasions as if gods and the goddesses are summoned in a special way to make an appearance to the devotees worshipping.

Swarnai

Swar-nai, a 'sushir vadya', holds an important place in the folk music of Kashmir. This instrument has been mentioned in Nilamata Purana and in Kalhana's Raj Tarangini. Swarnai holds the same place in Kashmir folk music as the Shahnai in the Indian music. This is the reason, why Swarnai is also called Shahnai in Kashmiri music.

Swar-nai is made of two words—Swar and Nai. The structure of Swarnai is slightly bigger in size as compared to Shahnai. This instrument is made of wood and its makers are the traditional makers of Swarnai. It has nine holes, near the round mouth of Swarnai, there is a tili type square, through which the player blows the air. This is also called Tulbarabir Tulkarav, in Kashmiri language.

The playing of Swarnai is considered very auspicious in Kashmiri culture. This musical instrument is deeply related to marriages, festivals, shivratri, navreh, Id and other auspicious occasions of Hindus as well as Muslims. It is also used by bhands while performing in folk drama—'Lok Natya'. Besides this, it is also widely used in 'bachi naghma' folk dance. During the harvest, the players of Swarnai go to farms and perform entertaining music to entertain the farmers and collect the crop for themselves.

This way, melodious Swarnai is widely used in the folk music culture of Kashmir.

Khasya

In Kashmiri folk music, round cup made of bronze is called khos'. Usually khos is used for drinking Kahva (a type of Kashmiri tea) in Kashmiri Hindu families. Beneath the round form of Khos is smaller round portion on which it stands. Khasya is the plural form of Khos. Whenever there is a religious gathering, marriage or yagnopavit, Tumbaknar, Ghat, two Khasya are played with both the hands. The Hindu women are more proficient in playing it. It is a 'Ghan Vadya'. The sound is produced by striking both the Khasya with each other.

Thaluz

Thaluz is a Kashmiri word. The instrument is called by different names in different regions of north and south—Jhanjh, Jhalari, Manjir, Thali Kans, Kanjaam, Illatalam, etc.

This instrument can be seen in temples of north and south during religious prayers in the mornings.

Kashmiri Thaluz is made of bronze, its round portion is around 13 cms. 30 cms. It is widely used in the folk functions of Kashmir. Thaluz is mentioned in Kalhana's Raj tarangini and Nilamata Purana. The use of instrument is mainly confined to the temples. On Saturday nights, in temples of Kashmir, usually 'Jagrans' are performed and many musical groups do kirtans, the whole night. Thaluz is then played by the performers, to summon the diety in invocation to the place of worship.

Rabab

The word 'Rabab' is pronounced as Rabab in Persian and Rabab in Arabic, which in Arabic is Rab-O-Raba; literary meaning to collect, to make available, to arrange or to manage.

It has been controversial to assert about the origin of Rabab, which was however initially played with a bow but now it is played with a mizrab precisely with a plectrum.

One school of thought suggests that this instrument has been brought to India from the middle East by the foreign intruders perhaps by Sokandar Zulqurmein in the past. Others suggest that Tansen, the celebrated musician invented it, as is mentioned in Ain-i-Akbari. Abu Naser-farabi is of the opinion that this instrument, originally played with a bow, was in fact successfully tried and played with a mizrab later on, in Middle East. One more lover and thinker of music Aullya-Chalbi of Arabia is of the opinion that Rabab was made in Arabia by one Abdullah before the birth of Prophet Mohammad of Islam.

However, in the encyclopedia of music, by A-Lavience, Rabab is said to be an Indian musical instrument, which was existing before 5000 BC during the time of king Ravana and was then known as Ravanastram, the strings of which were made from the guts of deer. Again, one more English author Rawlinson has written in his book 'ancient Monarchies' that Rabab was made in Iran. Nothing can be said authentically about its origin but it is one of the oldest stringed musical instruments known in the field of music, though it has undergone many changes in its form, structure and manner of playing.

The present day Rabab is made of seasoned mulberry wood. It is about three to three and a half feet in length. One end of the body is round and the diameter is about a foot. The round part is covered with parchment. This round part gradually joins the neck by becoming curved and narrow.

A piece of very thin wood is fixed at the top of the open part to cover it that serves the purpose of the fingerboard of the instrument. Four guts of different thickness are used in it as strings, in place of metal strings. The entire body of instrument is hollow from inside. It is played with a plectrum made of coconut shell, bone or of any hard metal.

Noet

It is a simple earthenware pot, usually for collection of water in rural India. Now a days it is usually made of brass or copper, but for musical purposes only the earthenware pot is traditionally used in Kashmiri music. It has a big round belly having a small open round mouth at the upper portion. It is the oldest type of drum variety known to the mankind.

In shape, the Noet of Kashmir is not different from the Ghatam of the South or the Matki of Rajasthan. They are used as the instruments in the music in those states which proves the fact that they might have begun their journey from the same cultural background. Their skill and style of playing might have differed in accordance with the traditions prevalent in respective regions.

In Kashmiri language, the original words 'Kalash' or 'Ghat' might have lost their existence and Noet might have gained popularity due to the fact that it was associated with 'uV'(nat). in due course of time the word 'nat kalash' might have lost the word 'kalash' and become popular as 'noet'. Such reference has been made in Nilamata Purana.

(i.e. reasted clay pot players—Bhands)

Kalhana in Raj Tarangini frequently refers to this instrument.

(they played on their balded heads exactly as the earthen pot instruments were played).

The tradition is maintained by the natives living in the distant rural areas of Kashmir, who spend their evenings in practicing this ancient art. The name of Mohan Lal Aima is worth mentioning here, who did a deep and thorough study of Noet playing and thus revived the art and its importance for us.

Nai (Flute)

In Kashmiri language, the normal meaning of 'Nai' is related to flute. In Kashmiri folk music, the prevalence of Nai is older than two thousand years as we get its description in Nilamata Purana.

"Punyahved shabdin vansi venurvenaya sut magadh shabden tatha vandisvanenc"

Nilamata Purana described banshi as well as venu and in the modern era even the Kashmiri artists, especially of Anantnag, are proficient in playing two types of flutes:

1. The first type of flute is empty from inside and there are seven holes for seven swaras. While playing it, fingers of both the hands are used. This type of flute is more prevalent in the folk life.
2. The second type of flute is also called 'Pi-Pi' in Kashmiri language. This type of flute is made of walnut's wood. Even this flute has seven holes

but the hole from where the air is blown is absent, but its adjacent hole is put into the mouth and blown. The player sees the seven holes clearly. This instrument is used more conveniently and the player does not get tired soon. This type of flute is more famous in Kashmir.

Santoor

Among the musical instruments, Santoor occupies an important place in Kashmiri music. Soofiana singing is not possible without its accompaniments. These days, it is joining popularity even outside Kashmir. Its sweet tappings create a feeling of romantic mood whereas its soft tunes remind of the transquality of the other world, which suits the mysticial temperament of soofiana music. This instrument emits loud and enchanting sounds. It requires subtle sense of turning on the part of the musicians who play it, with both hand using two sticks of twenty four centimeters called 'Kalam'. It is debatable whether Santoor is a native instrument of Kashmir or has been brought from abroad. Opinions differ. Some scholars view that it belongs to Iran. Pt. Shiv Kumar Sharma claims that he was the first ever Santoor maestro who brought it to classical stage. Santoor is being used for mousiqui in Kashmir since thirteenth century. But, that does not prove the fact that it came from abroad and its origin could not be Kashmir thirteen centuries before Christ. Reference to Shat-tantri veena is available at several places. It might have been the original form of Santoor and in due course, might have changed to the present form. The technique of performance, linguistically analyzing 'Shat' word must have traveled to 'Sat' and then to 'Sant; and 'tantri' to 'tantar' to 'trir' and finally to 'toor'. Both together must have become 'Santoor'. Had it been from foreign origin, it would have brought the name along.

Santoor is made of mulberry wood. Some scholars

believe it to be related to Shakt sect. According to Shakts, triangular is a symbol of desire, knowledge and action.

They have referred to the Shakt instruments, several times, and believed that goddess Mahashakti should be worshipped accompanying these instruments. The base on which Santoor is placed is also the same shape.

Mulberry tree in Kashmir has a religious value. It is related to 'Bhairav'. In every 'Bhairav' temple, mulberry tree is parted with vermilion and people worship it devotedly. In Khirbhavani, the famous Shakt pilgrimage, the goddess is sitting on the mulberry tree. The very pilgrimage is called 'tulnuri' meaning 'root of mulberry'.

The shape of Santoor is trapezoid. Its right side is called 'burn' and the left 'Jil'. Twelve wires on right side are of brass and those on the left are of iron. There are also twelve nobs on the right and twelve on the left side. Four wires are fixed to each nob. The production of the tune depends on the nobs. Twelve brass wires remind us of soft and sweet Shakt emotion and the throbbing tune of iron wires remind us of hard appearance of Shiva himself. The number of wires in total is ninety six. At the tune of yagnopavit, the priest wraps the holy thread ninety six times around his palm. The number is significant in itself. The tops of the nobs are inlaid in the horns of stag. This animal is found in Kashmir alone.

Twentieth century leading player of Santoor has been Tibat Bakal. At present Saz Naivaz, Kaleem, Shekh Abdul Aziz are known for their style of playing. Pandit Bhajan Sopori is making it popular on classical stage and popularizing it all over the world.

Saaz-i-Kashmir

Saaz had not originated from Kashmir. Since it has remained in vogue in Kashmir for centuries without any major modification, people preferred to call it Saaz-i-Kashmir or the musical instrument devised in Kashmir. It is played with bow, as such it is easier for the player to get microtones out of it.

According to Rouhulla Khalighi, Saaz in Persia is called Kamancha. It is the same instrument called Saaz in Kashmir and is played by a bow. He again states that the instrument has now been replaced by the violin as it is more complete. There are very few people who can play the Kamancha now-a-days.

Saaz is found all over the Islamic world and it originated from the north Iranian district, Kudristan. This type of instrument (Three stringed fiddle) is mentioned as early as the tenth century AD, by the great theorist Al Farabi. The instrument is found elsewhere in the Middle east also. Since the Kashmir Saaz is more developed and complicated, that is why people have named it as Saaz-i-Kashmir. The Iranian use this instrument for vocal accompaniment.

Saaz-i-Kashmir has three prominent strings, two made of silk. The silk string is made worthy of producing musical sound by mixing it with the skin of fish. It is tuned to Sa, while the 2nd one is tuned to SA (middle octave). The third one is not made use of, as it is not touched by the bow. On either side of the dand, there are seven strings (right side) made of steel and seven strings (left side) made of brass. Right side resonance strings are tuned respectively from Pa to Ma, whereas that of the left side from Sa to Ni (middle octave).

Setar/Sehtar

The invention of Sitar is commonly credited to Amir Khusrau, scholars, generally, refer to him as the originator of Indian Classical Sitar. Some others are of the opinion that musicians adopted Tritantri Veena and improved upon it and created Sitar. The theory which is widely accepted is that Sehtar was the instrument brought by Amir Khusrao from Iran. According to Bimal Mukherjee (The History and Origin of Sitar), by the 11th or 12th century the second Sitar had emerged, an instrument, to accompaniment to vocal music and later also as an independent instrument. A little later there was a series of Muslim invasions on north. The invaders mostly Persians and Turks, were not only brave warriors but also loved finer things of life like music. Some of them had brought along with a small instrument with three strings called Sehtar, meaning three strings. Even Abul Fazal says that another instrument called Been was like Yantra and contained three strings.

Probably the word Sitar is derived from this Sehtar. The Sitar which resembles the Persian Tambura or ud, in shape, and the Indian Veena, in principle, is itself a fusion and an epitome of the Indo-Persian culture and civilization.

Despite this opinion, same authors say that it is a gradual process of development from Tritantri Veena. Others say that the invention of Sitar is attributed to Amir Khusrao and that is probably of Persian origin. Kashmiri Sehtar or Sitar is said to be original model of Indian Sitar. This instrument is now however, comparable to Indian Sitar of these days and retains its originality. The Kashmiri Sehtar is the original instrument accompanying Sufiana Kalaam or Mousiqui which came to Kashmir from Central Asia.

Sitar is a long neck plucked lute, similar to the Persian Sitar. Curt Sach is of the view that the Arabs call it the largest variety. 'Tanbur Kabir Turki' or large Turkish lute. The Persian, however, do not use the word Tunbur and they designate the stringed instrument by the word Tar. This is why the people mostly called it Persian Sitar. This type of Sehtar or Sitar was widely used in Kashmir. In villages (especially in Wahthora, where jesters called Bhand live) Sufiana musicians would use Kashmiri Sitar for accompaniment of this Mousiqui. This musical instrument is specially meant for accompaniment purpose for Sufiana

Mousiqui unlike the Indian Sitar which is used for solo purpose only. Gradually the Sitar had come to acquire five strings by stages and the number has recently increased to seven strings. The structure of Kashmiri Sitar is as under: it has Dand which in some is 2· wide over which frets made of threads are fixed, a Tumba which is either made of wood or that of gourd. Tumba is about one third to one fourth of the size of Indian Sitar (Tumba).

Wasul/Dokra/Tabla

Wasul or Dokra is the only percussion instrument used in Sufiana Mousiqui. Wasul is a double membrane barrel shaped drum used in Sufiana Kalam, until some seventy years ago. It is played in a manner similar to Tabla and provides the rhythm of Maqamat in Sufiana Mousiqui. About a decade ago, the Research Library Srinagar, published two manuscripts of music (Tarana Saroor and Karamat-i-Mujra) with some old paintings of musicians. One such painting was printed opposite maqam-i-Dhanasri. This painting has pictures of:

1. Two Hafizas dancers wearing Peshwaz (special dress in Kashmir for both male and female dancers).
2. Two musicians with a Sitar and Tabla type Wasul.
3. Two musicians, one carrying Sitar.

This clearly shows that Wasul had been in use as Rhythm instrument earlier to Tabla and had primacy over Tabla.

Originally Tabla had some other shape and was called Mridanga. Mridanga is accompanied with the Carnatic music. Later on, Mridanga was divided into two pieces and after undergoing modification it became the modern Tabla.

Under the later Indian influence Wasul or Dokra was completely substituted and replaced by Indian Tabla. Tabla has been found to be more convenient, easier and a suitable instrument as compared to Wasul. Sufiana Musicians have completely given up Dokra or Wasul and have adopted Tabla. Therefore, there is hardly any person who knows the playing of these instruments, as they have become totally extinct.

4

Some Famous Songs with Text and Notation

Hindu Vanvun

Text

शोकलम करिथ वनवुन ह्योतुये
शोभफल धुतुय माजि भवाने
कनि दान कोरनय नारायनो
भूमि दान रोटुथो ब्राह्मनो !

The first line begins with the prayer to Lord Ganesha for His benign grace. Blessings, for the occasion are expected from goddess Bhavani. The next line describes about the Kanyadaan being performed by the father and offerings received by the Brahmins on the occasion of girl's marriage.

Notation: **(Raga Des)**

सा	नि	स	–,	रे	स	ऩिसा,	
शोक	ल	ऽ	म,	क	ऽ	रिथ	
ऩि	सा	–	ऩि	–	ऩिसा	–	
व	न	ऽ	वुन,	ह्योतु	ये	ऽ	
स	ऩि	सा	–,	रे	–	सा	ऩिसा,
शो	भ	ऽऽ	फ	ऽऽ	ल	ऽऽ	धुतुय

निसा	—	ऩिस	ऩिसा	—	सा		
माजि	ऽऽ	भवां	ऽऽ	ने	ऽ		
सा	ऩि	सा	ऩि	सा	ऩिऩि	रे	सा
क	ऩि	ऽऽ	दान	ऽऽ	कोर	न	ऽ
ऩि	सा	नि	सा	ऩि	सा	ऩि	सऩि
य	ना	ऽऽ	रा	ऽऽ	य	नो	ऽऽ

Muslim Vanvun

Text

जीप छय सोनसंज़
हैडल संग लातुक
आवय जंगलातुक तहसीलदार,
बूटस प्यठ छुय पतलून नारिए
च़ कसू पअरिए आश्कि गोख,

This marriage chorus is sung by Muslim women at the time of girl's marriage. The lines are addressed to the bridegroom who is arriving. These lines imply that the jeep in which the bridegroom is coming is made of gold and its handle is made of iron. The groom seems to be looking like the 'Tehsildaar' (the Tehsildaar held the position of the king of the area). He is coming from the jungle. Next line gives the description of his shoes and pants. He is looking gorgeous and has been enchanted by the beauty of the fairy, i.e. the bride.

Notation: **(Raga Todi)**

स	रे	ग	रे	ग	रे	रे	ग	रे	सा	—	—
जीऽ	प	छय	सोन	सऽन	ज़	है	डल	संग	ला	ऽ	तुक
×			0			×			0		
स	रे	ग	ग	रेसा	रे	रे	ग	रे	सा	—	—
आ	वय	जंग	ला	ऽऽ	तुक	ते	ऽ	सिल	दा	ऽ	र
×			0			×			0		

स	रे	ग	रे	ग	रे	रे	ग	रे	सा	—	—
बू	ऽ	टस	पै	ठई	छुई	पत	लू	न	ना	रि	ए
×			0			×			0		
स	रे	मं	ग	रेस	रे	रे	ग	रे	सा	—	—
च़	क	सू	प	अ	रिए	आ	ऽ	शिक	गो	ऽ	ख
×			0			×			0		

Veegya Vacchan

Text:

हअर वछुम नच़ने
सअर सोन्सुन्दये
हारि गछ़ि डेजुहर,
सुति सोनसुन्दये
हारि गछ़ि हल्क बंद
सुति सोन्सुन्दये
हारि गछ़ि चन्दन हार
सुति सोन्सुन्दये

This folk song is sung at the time of marriage and yagnopavit. The love and affection of the mother-in-law for her daughter-in-law is shown in these lines. The mother-in-law wants to gift various gold ornaments to her daughter-in-law and calls her a nightingale, out of affection.

Notation:

सासा	रेरे	रेग	रेरे	सासा	सासा	रेरे	सा—
हअर	वछ़म	नच़	नेऽ	सऽर	सोन	सुन्द	ये ऽ
सासा	रेरे	रेग	रेरे	सासा	सासा	रेरे	सा—
हारि	गछ़ि	डेजु	हर	सुति	सोन	सुन्द	ये ऽ
सासा	रेरे	रेग	रेरे	सासा	सासा	रेरे	सा—
हारि	गछ़ि	चन्दन	हार	सुति	सोन	सुन्द	ये ऽ

Text:

हुम वोथुम वीग्य खोतुम
तोत वथुम यार बल

The lad is affectionately addressed as the 'Parrot', who has been taken to the river after the yagnopavit.

Notation:

रे	रे	रे	रे	ग	ग	ग	ग
हु	म	वोथु	म	ब	गि	खो	तुम

रे	रे	रे	रे	ग	ग	ग	रे
तो	त	वोथु	म	या	र	ब	ल

Ruf

Text:

गोम चे़य पथ लौकचारय, पत लारय मदनो
नाद लायय दर बारय, पत लारय मदनो
छुय न इन्सान बेआरय, पत लारय मदनो
जान वन्दयो जानि जानै पत लारय मदनो
छुरव बेयन खोत प्यदि शानो, पत लारय मदनो
नाद लायय दरबारय, पत लारय मदनो

This is 'RUF'. The lady is showing utter sacrifice for the lost lover. He has gone to some far-off country. If he continues to do so then she will forgo all social traditions and follow him wherever he is. She has sacrificed her entire youth for his sake.

Notation:

सासा	रेरे	सासा	सा	रेरे	सासा	सासा	रेरे	गरे	रे	सा	सा–
गोम	चे़य	पत	लौक	चाऽ	रय	पत	लाऽ	रय	मद	नोऽ	ऽऽ

सासा	रेरे	सासा	सा	रेरे	सासा	सासा	रेरे	गरे	रे	सा	सा–
नाद	लाऽऽ	यय	दर	बा	रय	पत	लाऽऽ	रय	मद	नो	ऽऽ

सासा	रेरे	सारा	सा	रेरे	सासा	सासा	रेरे	गरे	रे	सा	सा–
पान	माऽ	रान	खून	हा	रान	पत	लाऽऽ	रय	मद	नो	ऽऽ

Hikat Gyavun

Text:

हतबी ब्यनी, क्या बी ब्यनि
यिमा वुछ बोने, बोऽय म्योन
हलि क्याह, शुगल म्योन!
नल्य क्याह, पोछ़ म्योन
खोरन क्याह, लचिदार पाज़ार
गछ़ बा गछ़, हब्ब कदल वास
तति म्यानि व्यस, यिय शूबयस
कलमदानस काकलालस, हक्कची, हक्कची ची

The song is sung by small girls while playing. The love of brother and sister is reflected in this song. The brother has disappeared. The sister asks other friends, if any one of them has seen her brother.

Notation:

सा	रे	सा	सा	सा	रे–	सा	नि
हत	बी	ब्य	नी	क्या	बी	ब्य	नी
सा	रे	सा	सा	सा	रे–	सा	नी
यि	मा	वुछ	वोन	बो	य	म्यो	न
सा	रे	सा	–	स–	रे	सा–	–
ह	लि	क्या	ऽ	शुग	ल	म्यो	न
सा	रे	सा	–	सा–	रे	सा–	–
ना	ल्य	क्या	ऽ	पो	छ	म्यो	न

Van

Text:

काक गव पानय सौरगय अन्दर
नौशि कोरि अनिनय क्या सौन्दर
लरि जायि लज़नय क्या सौन्दर
वेदा परिनय क्या सौन्दर

The dead person is praised for his achievements while living.

Notation:

रे	रे	ग	ग	ग	म	ग	–
काक	गव	पा	नय	सौर	गय	अन	दर
ग	ग	रे	रे	ग	ग	रे	–
लरि	जायि	लज़	नय	क्या	ऽ	सौन्	दर

Lalnavun

Text

ब बन्द आसिथ शरमन्द थवनस
गजिसो ब च्यानि अमार लालो, ज़न्नत दोज़क
चे़ति स्वरिथ गोरव, मरिथ यिमयनो दुबार लालो
बन्द असिथ शरमन्द थवनस, वानिच औसस चन्दनदारो
तति म्य वोतुम तबरदारो, चतिथ ब त्रावनस होरिवथ ज़ऽजनस
ग़जिसो ब च्याने अमार लो लो ज़री जामन नरिय वऽथय चाव परी
लागय खरीदारो

The first line perhaps implies that the child is a priceless gift of God, which has put the mother to shame, i.e. she feels overwhelmed by his bounty. This song embodies a mixture of many shades of thought and feeling—Sufi mysticism, fondling of the child by the mother and attitude to God.

Notation

प़प़	–प	धध	सा	प़प़	–प	धध	सासा
बब	ऽन्द	आसि	थ	शरम	ऽन्द	थव	नस
गजि	ऽसो	बच्या	नि	अमा	ऽर	ला	लो

The mother addresses the darling child that he is as precious for her as the earring hanging in her ear. She will make him swing in the cradle and the cradle will swing like a lady's ear ring.

Text

गूर गूर करयो कनके दूरो, कनके दूरो!
टयन्ड़य मा ददियो मरगै चूरो मरगै चूरो
सुन क्याह खयो ढूल ज़म्बूरो ढूल ज़म्बूरो
दिलि हन्दि शाहज़ाद आख लूहरो आख लोहूरो!
च्योन म्ये दूर्यर छुमहो सूरो छुमहो सूरो
मुलवथ बाज़ार हटि हन्जूरो, हटि हन्जूरो
अश्कै नारन कोरमो सूरो, कोरमो सूरो
मय मारमति म्ये चावतो पूरो चावतो पूरो
महमूद गामी चृन्दन दूरो चृन्दन दूरो

Notation: **(Raga Bilawal)**

प	प	प	म	गरि	–	स–	गग	रिगरे	सासा	रे	गप–
गू	र	गू	र	कर	ऽ	योऽ	कन	के–	–दू	–	रो–

म	गरि	सा	––	ग	रि	स	पप	–प	म	गरि–	स–
ऽ	कन	के	ऽऽ	दू	ऽ	रो	टयन्ड़य	मा	द	दिऽ	योऽ

–	गग	रेगरे	सा	सा	रे	गप	–म	गरिस	––	ग ग	रे–
ऽ	मर	गै	ऽ	चू	रो	––	ऽ–	मरगै	ऽऽ	चूरो	ऽ–

Ladishah

Text:

हवाई जहाज़ आव मुल्क कशमीर
यिमव वुछ तिमव कोर तोब तकसीर

The song depicts the reaction of the public in Kashmir on seeing the aeroplane for the first time.

Notation:

ध़ध़ध़	ध़ध़ध़	ध़ध़	ध़—
हवाई जहाज़	आवय	मुल्कि	कशमीर
ध़ध़ध़	ध़ध़ध़	ध़ध़	ध़—
चिमव वुछ	तिमव कोर	तोब	तकसीर

Chhakar

Text

हअरिये थावकना कन त लोलो
ज़ार म्यान तोतस वन्त लोलो
मदनस वनतय अनतस आऽर
वदनस छुम न ज़ाह त, च़्यन त लोलो
बादाम चश्मय मअच़रावान
तन छुम मअक्षराण्यन त लोलो
सिल मे कोरनम् कानि दवन
सोत छम पाम दिवान त लोलो

These lines depict the agony of a young lady whose lover has gone away. The background shows various plants, trees and water-falls where she is giving vent to such feelings and also refers to the taunts she has to bear from another lady in her man's life. The 'Parrot' has been used as a metaphor for the lover.

***Notation:* (Raga Jaijaiwanti)**

स	–	–	रे	रे	ग॒	ग॒	रे
हा	रि	ये	ऽ	ऽ	ऽ	थ	वक
सा	नि़	स	–	रे	–	सा	–
ना	ऽ	कन	त	लो	ऽ	लो	ऽ
स	–	सा	रे	रे	ग॒	ग॒	रे
ज़ा	र	म्य	ऽ	ऽ	न	तो	ऽ
सा	नि़	सा	–	रे	–	सा	–
तस	ऽ	वन	त	लो	ऽ	लो	ऽ
प	प	प	ध	प	म	ग	–
म	द	न	ऽ	ऽ	स	वन	ऽ
ग	–	म	प	ध	–	प	–
त	स	अन	ऽ	त	स	आ	र

Text:

ललि ललि नोवुमै अमार
अज़हय आव पान बालियार
तिपल द्राव म्योन लोकचार
अज़हय आव पान बालयार
व्यसिये छुमै चिकचाव
महाराज़ म्योन हाई आव

This song is sung at the time of girl's marriage. The enthusiasm of the girl at the time of the arrival of the bridegroom is depicted in these lines. She is addressing her friends that her early youth has been full of excitement and fervour and the day has finally come when the bridegroom is arriving.

Notation:

रे रे	सनि़	सा–	सा–	रे–	ग
ललि	ललि	नो	वुमै	अमा	र
रे रे	सनि़	सा–	रे रे	सा–	सा–
अज़हय	आव	पान	बाल	या	र
रे रे	सांनि़	सा–	रे रे	सा–	सा–
अज़हय	आव	पान	बाल	या	र
रे रे सानि़	सांनि़	सा–	सा–	रे	ग
व्यसि	ये	छुमै	चिक	चा	व
रे रे	सानि़	सा	रे रे	सा–	सा–
महा	राज	म्योन	हाई	आ	व

Text

करसऽ म्योन न्याय अन्दे मऽर मन्दे मदनवारो
बाल कअड़थस गटे, हटे तल के मोख्तहारौ
गन्ड़ हाऽथ अकि लटे मऽर मन्दे मदनवारो
शबे अकि यूरियितम यार म्याने सितम्बगारो
रेशे दीदार दितम् मऽर मन्दे मदनवारो
सौन छम पाम् दिवान्
कलि देव जानावारो तनै बोतुम वदान्।

The song is romantic. The lover has been separated from the beloved, who has since been shedding tears and listening to the taunts given by the 'other lady' of the man. The value of the lover for the beloved is as precious as the pearl garland.

Notation: **(Raga Des)**

रे	ग	रे	ऩि	सा	रे	ग	रे	सा	सा	सा	सा
कर	सा	म्यो	न	न्या	ऽ	य	अन	दे	ऽ	ऽ	ऽ

रे–	ग	म–	गरे	सा	–	सा	सा	रेग	–	रे	सा
मऽर	मन	दे	ऽऽ	ऽऽ	म	द	न	वा	रो	ऽ	ऽ

पध	पम	गग	रेरे	सा	–	–	–
बाल	कड़	थड	सग	टे	ऽ	ऽ	ऽ

रे–	ग	मम	गरे	सा	सा	सा	–	सा	रे–	गरे	सा
हटि	तल	केऽ	ऽऽ	मो	ख	त	ऽ	हा	रो	ऽ	ऽ

रे	ग	रे	ऩि	सा	रे	ग	रे	–	–	–	–
ग	न्ड़	ह	त	अकि	ऽ	ऽ	ल	टे	ऽ	ऽ	ऽ

Soofiana

Text:

म्योनुय वनतस हा वने हऽरी
म्योनुय वनतस हा वने हऽरी
असि छु ताशोक लगव यऽरी
म्योनुय वनतस हाऽ वने हारी
यूर्यरव अनतन वनहऽस ब ज़ारी
असि छु ताशोक ल यऽरी

The mistress is addressing her friend "Tell him of me, O friend nymph! We would join friendship. Bring Him here. Tell Him of me. Bring Him here. I would offer my lamentation to Him."

Notation:

स	सस	रेरे	गग	–म	पध	नि	सं	––
म्यो	नुय	वन	तस	ऽहा	बने	हऽ	री	ऽऽ

नि	निनि	धध	पप	–ध	प ध	नि	सं	– –
म्यो	नुय	वन	तस	ऽहा	व ने	हऽ	री	ऽऽ
निनि	ध	नि	संरेसं	नि ध	प प	म	ग	– –
असि	छु	ता	शो	क ल	ग व	या	ऽ	रीऽ
स	सस	रेरे	गग	–म	पप	ध	नि सं	– –
म्यो	नुय	वन	तस	ऽहा	वने	हाऽ	रीऽ	ऽऽ

Text:

यार यितम लगवो यारान तय, यारा यितम
यार यितम लागवो यारान तय, यार यितम
चोक छुस नालानतय शोक ध्याने

Lover is addressing the beloved "come O Beloved Join friendship with me. For thy love, my love is lamenting."

***Notation:* (Raga Durga)**

सस	रेम	मम	पप	धध	धप	
दिथ	वाजि	नस	नावि	लोलो	ऽ	
सासा	रेम	मम	मप	धध	धप	
दिथ	वाजि	नस	नावि	लोलो	ऽ	
धध	धप	मम	धप	पम	मम	मम
छुम	यार	माऽ	रावि	लोऽ	लोऽ	ऽऽ
सांसां	धप	मम	मप	धध	धप	मम
छुम	यार	माऽ	रावि	लोऽ	लोऽ	ऽऽ
पम	पध	सां	––	संरें	संसं	धप
ध–	पम...					

Bibliography

Noor Mohammad Bhat : *Sufiana Mousiqui,* Art Press, Red Cross Road, Srinagar, Kashmir.

Sulochana Brahaspati : *Khusrau Tansen Tatha Anya Kalakar,* Raj Kamal Prakashan, New Delhi, 1976.

Chand Khan, Hazrat Amir Khusrau : *Mausiqui Manzil Suyon Wala,* Delhi-6.

B.C. Dev : *Musical Instruments,* National Book Trust of India.

S.N. Dhar : *Jammu & Kashmir Folk Lore.*

J.C. Dutta : *Kings of Kashmira,* Translation Work of the Sanskrit Works of Kalhana, Jonaraja, Srivara, Calcultta.

Mohibul Hassan : *Kashmir under Sultan's,* Ali Mohammad & Son Publishers, Srinagar Kashmir, 1959.

Jonaraja : Zain Raj Tarangini, Translated by Dutta, J.C., *Kings of Kashmira.*

S.M. Ikram : *Muslim Civilization in India,* edited by Ainslie T. Embree, New York, Columbia, 1964.

Kamudi : *Kashmir its Cultural Heritage.*

Kalhana : Raj Tarangini, English Translation by M.A. Stein, London, *A Chronicle of the Kings of Kashmir.*

M.L. Kapur : *The History of Medievel Kashmir,* Jammu ARV Publicaton, 1971.

R.C. Kak : *Ancient Monuments of Kashmir,* Sripratap Museum, Srinagar, 1923.

Jawahar Lal Nehru : *Discovery of India,* Oxford University Press, 1988.

National Amir Khusrau Society : *Life Times and Works of Amirkhusrau.*

Mohammad Khan : *Gulam Mohammad and Sons,* Kashmiri Bazar, Lahore, Karachi.

M.L. Koul : *Kashmir Past and Present.*

Abdul Majid Mattoo : *Kashmir under the Mughals.*

Shyam Koul : *Agony of Kashmir.*

S.L. Pandit : *My Kashmir Diary.*

S.L. Sadhu : *Medievel Kashmir.*

Kamlakar Mishra : *Kashmir Saivism.*

Jaishree Kak Odin : *Laila's Life and Poetry.*

Swami Laxman Joo : *Kashmir Shaivism.*

S.L. Shali : *Kashmir History and Archaeology through the Ages.*

S.K. Ganjoo : *Kashmir Earliest Times of the Present Day.*

Bamzay, P.N. Koul : *History and Culture of Kashmir.*

P.N. Bazaz : *Struggle for Freedom in Kashmir.*

Abdul Ahad Azad : *Kashmiri Zuban Aur Shairi,* Srinagar Kashmir.

R.K. Razdan : *Kashmir Ki Lalit Kalayen.*

G.M.D. Sufi : *Islamic Culture in Kashmir,* University of Landen, Pakistan, 1949.

Abdul Haleem Shrar : *Hindustani Mausiqui.*

J.A. Subhan : *Sufism its Saints and Shrines,* Lucknow, 1960.

Abdul Azir Sheikh : *Koshur Sargam,* Volumes 3, Academy of Art Culture & Language, 1963, Srinagar.

P.V. Tickoo : *Story of Kashmir.*

Index

Studies in Theatre History and Culture
Edited by Heather Nathans